Gabi Wolf
MiniMania
⸱COLORING BOOK⸱
4

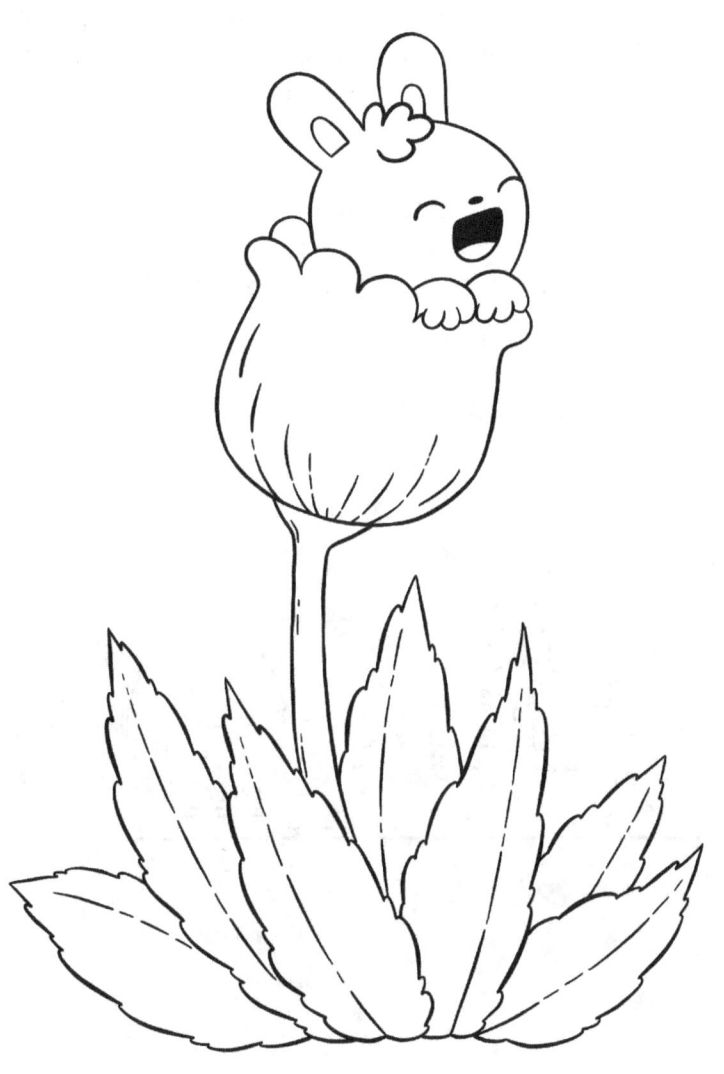

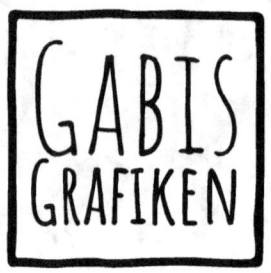

**Copyright © 2024 Gabi Wolf, Berlin
All rights reserved.**

All illustrations published in this book are protected by copyright and may only be used commercially with the express written permission of the author. Reproduction or distribution of the contents of the book , even for private purposes, is prohibited and will be prosecuted under civil and criminal law. This applies in particular to reproductions, translations, microfilms, and storage and distribution in electronic systems. The author disclaims any liability for damages of any kind or misuse of this book.

ISBN: 979-8321965856
Independently published
Cover & Illustrations: Gabi Wolf

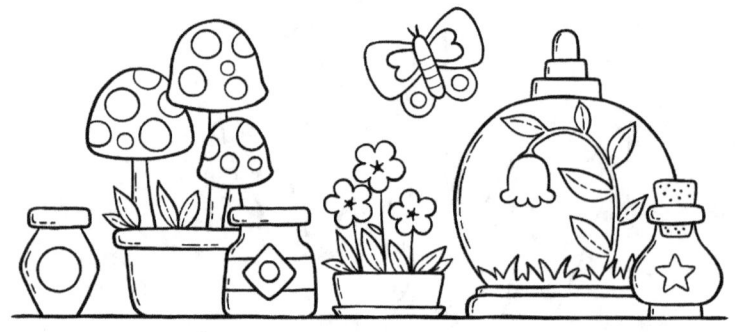

This book belongs to:

_____

_____

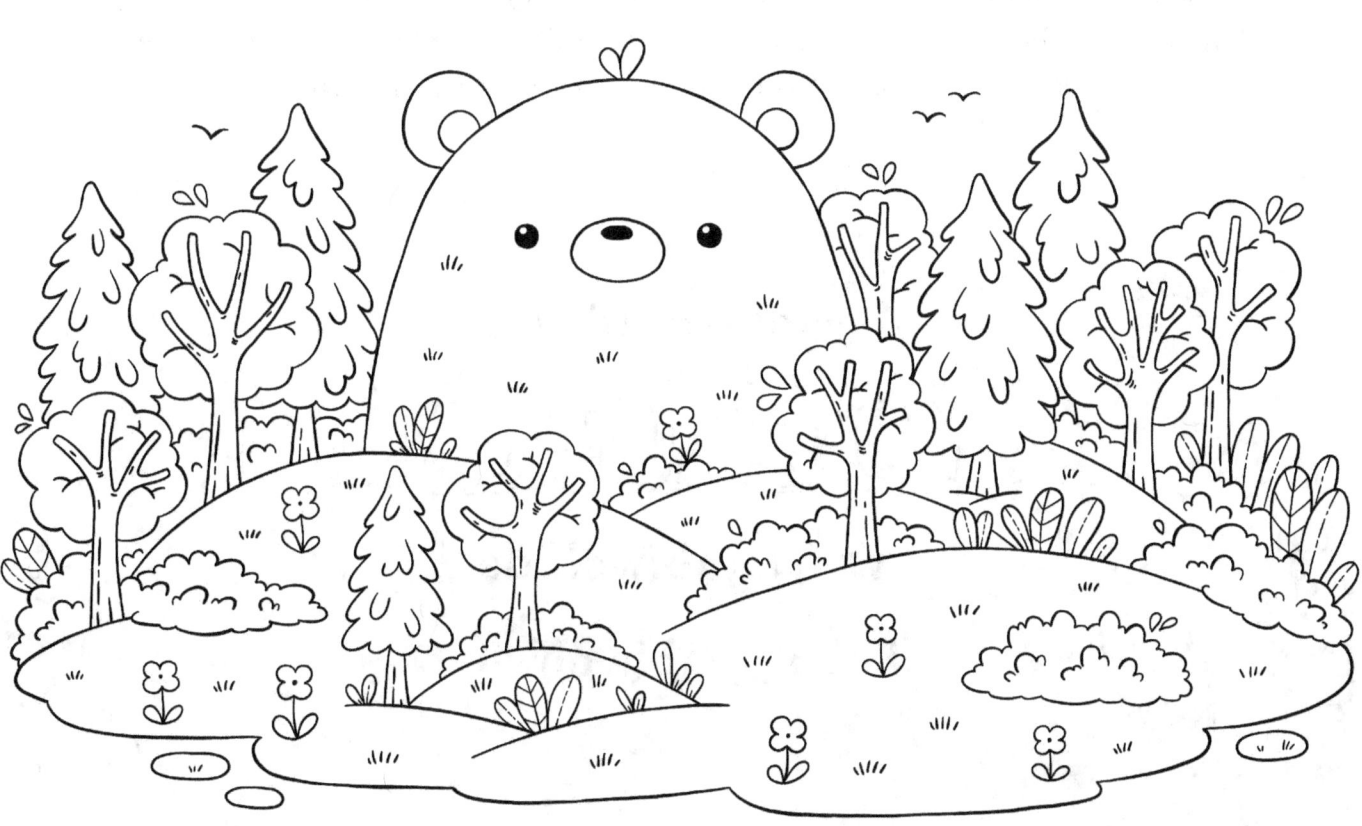

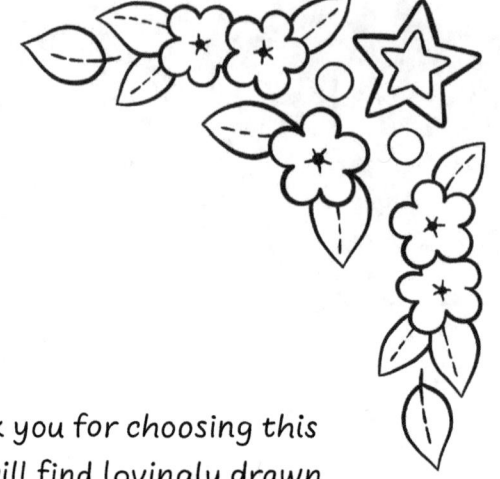

Welcome

Nice to have you here. First of all, I would like to thank you for choosing this coloring book. I really appreciate it. In this book you will find lovingly drawn coloring pictures from the sweet magical world of Minimania. Explore their secret worlds and bring them to life through color.

Once you have created your own personal work of art, I would be very happy if you shared it on social media. Please use #gabisgrafiken or @gabiwolf so that I can find your picture.

I'm also always happy to receive feedback on my books. This helps me make the next books even more varied and interesting. You can contact me via Instagram, Facebook, YouTube or email. I promise to reply to every message. Of course, I'm also happy to receive a review on Amazon.

@gabisgrafiken

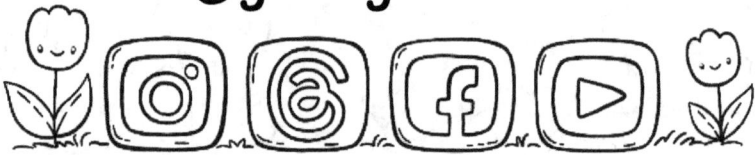

www.gabiwolf.de

hello@gabiwolf.de

Tips for Coloring

To make sure you have fun coloring, I recommend placing a few sheets of paper under the picture you're working on. This is a good base and prevents the color from pressing through or transferring to the page underneath.

If you want to use felt pens or watercolors, check them out first on the color test pages at the end of the book. This will tell you if too much of the paint has been applied and is visible through the paper. Don't paint over the same spot too many times in a row.

Of course, crayons are also great for coloring. They offer a wide variety of options by blending or applying in several layers. So you can achieve many wonderful effects.

The pages are printed on one side. So you can cut out pictures that you particularly like and hang them up.

And now I wish you lots of fun coloring.

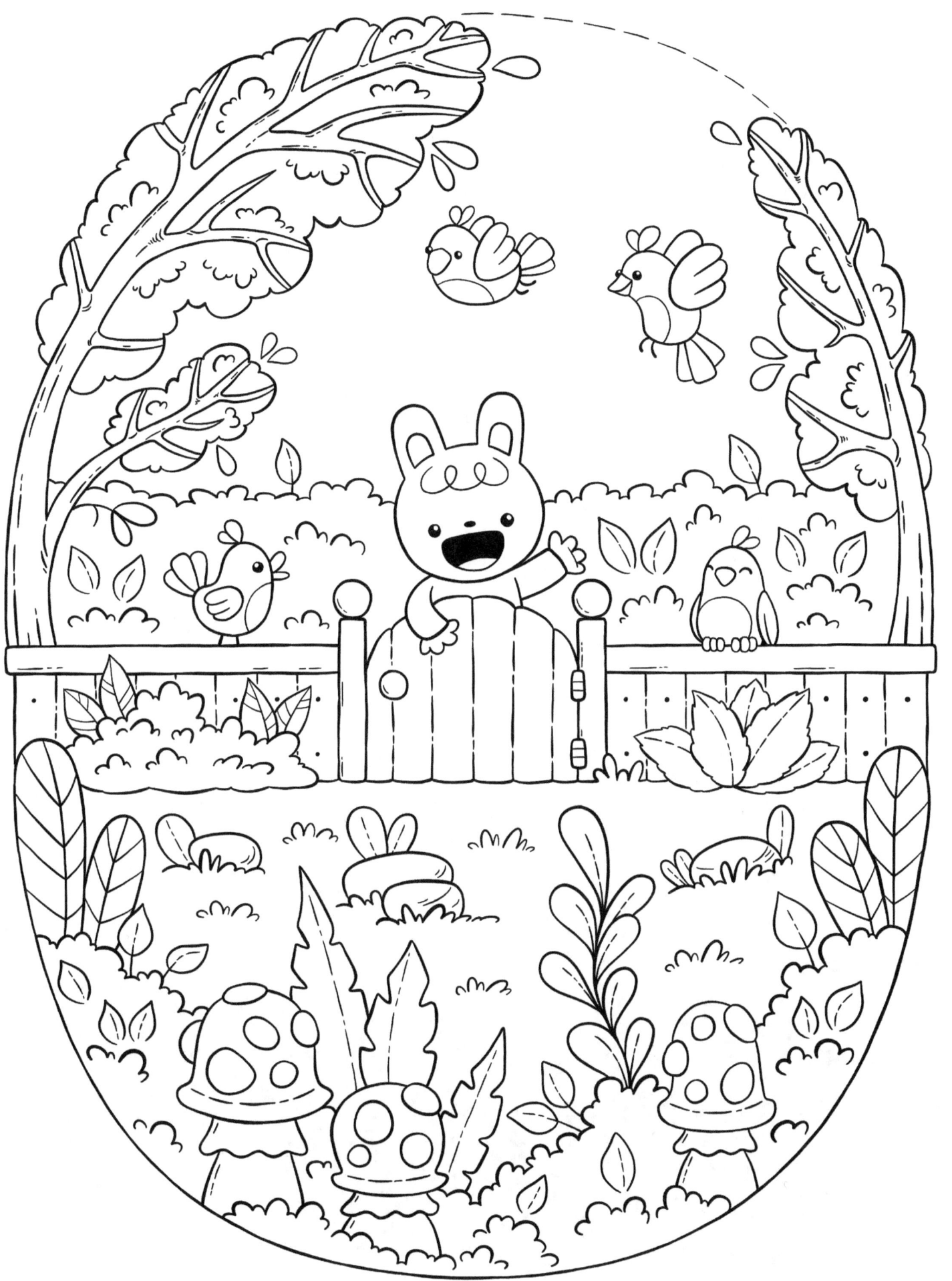

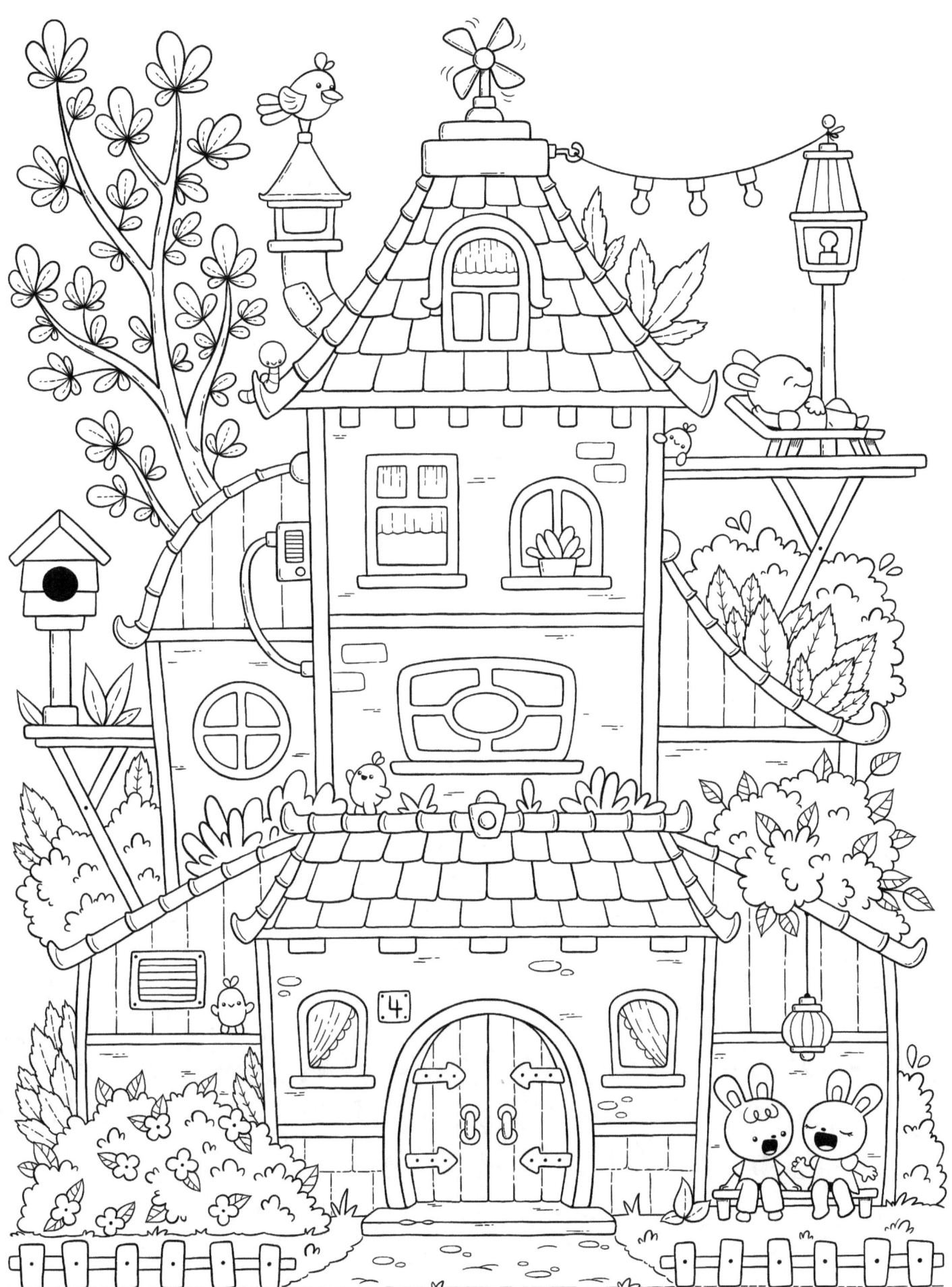

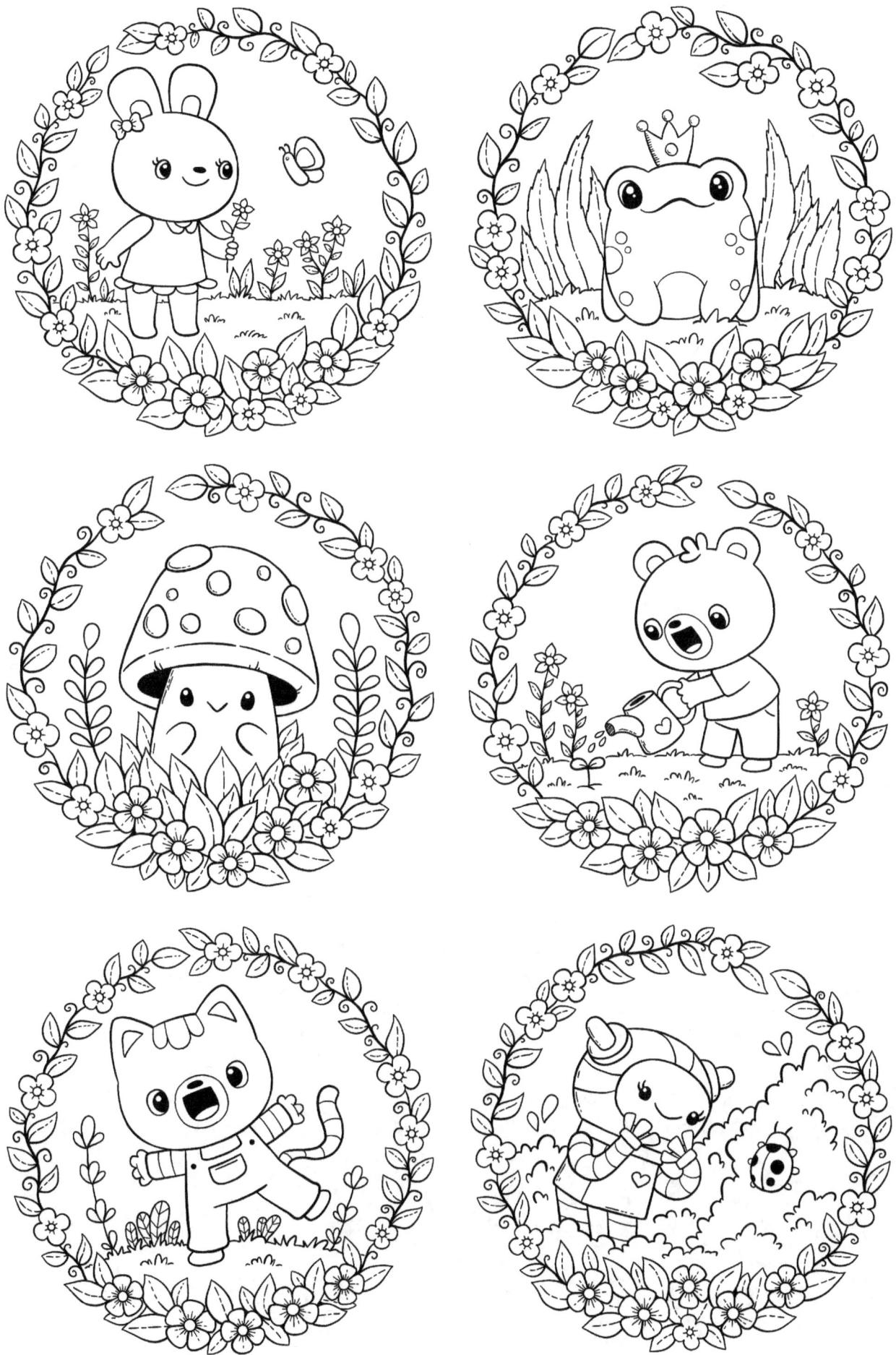

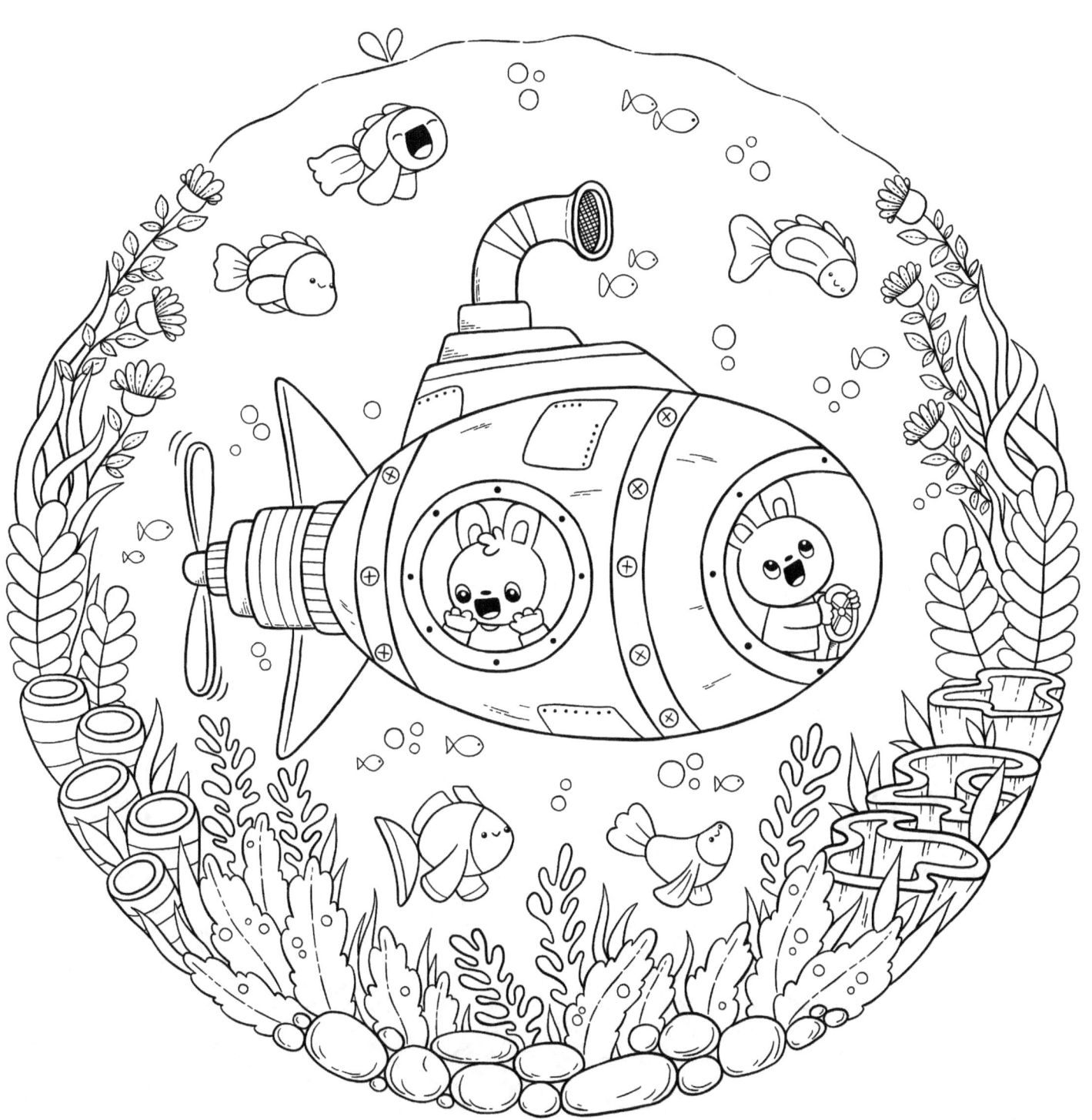

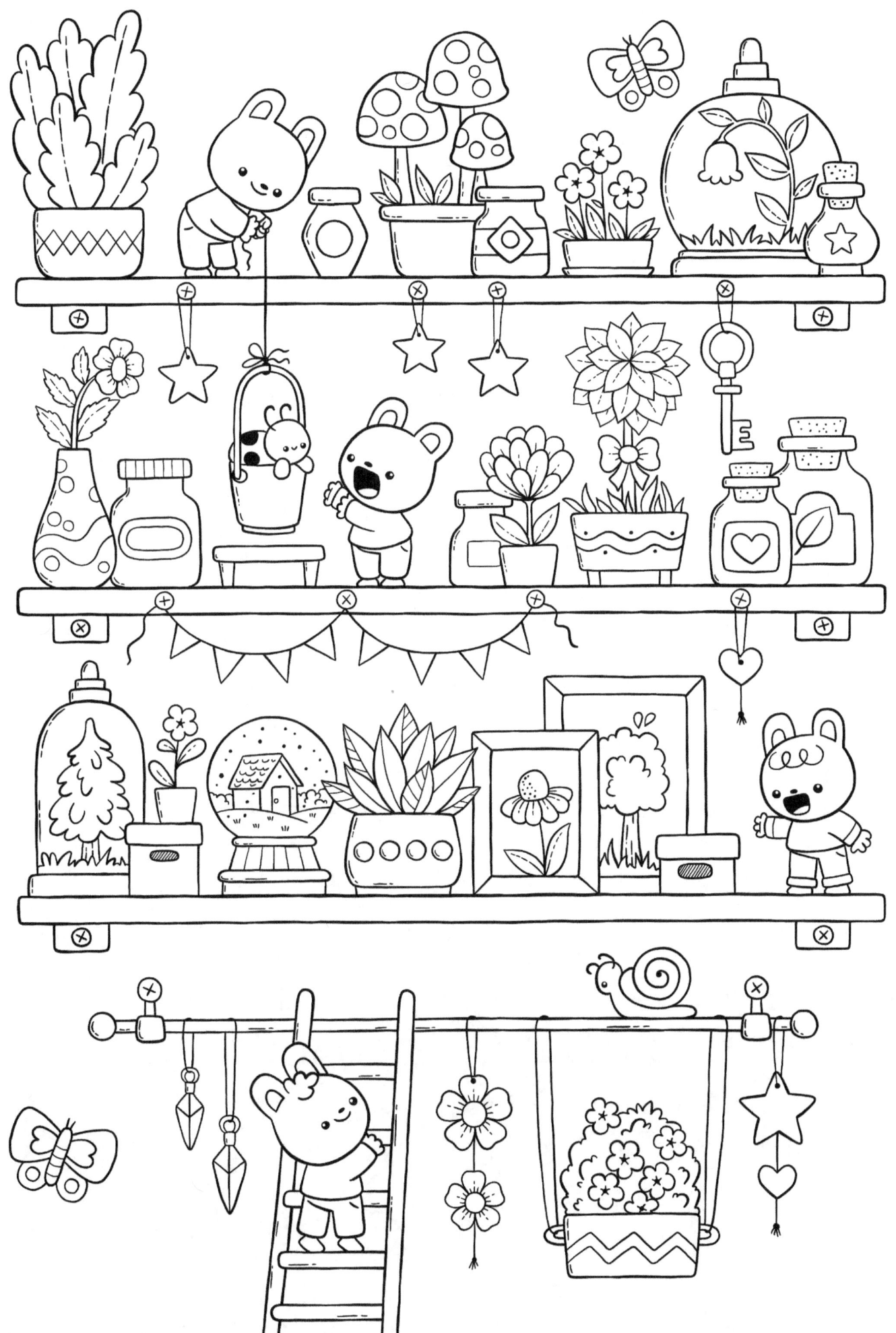

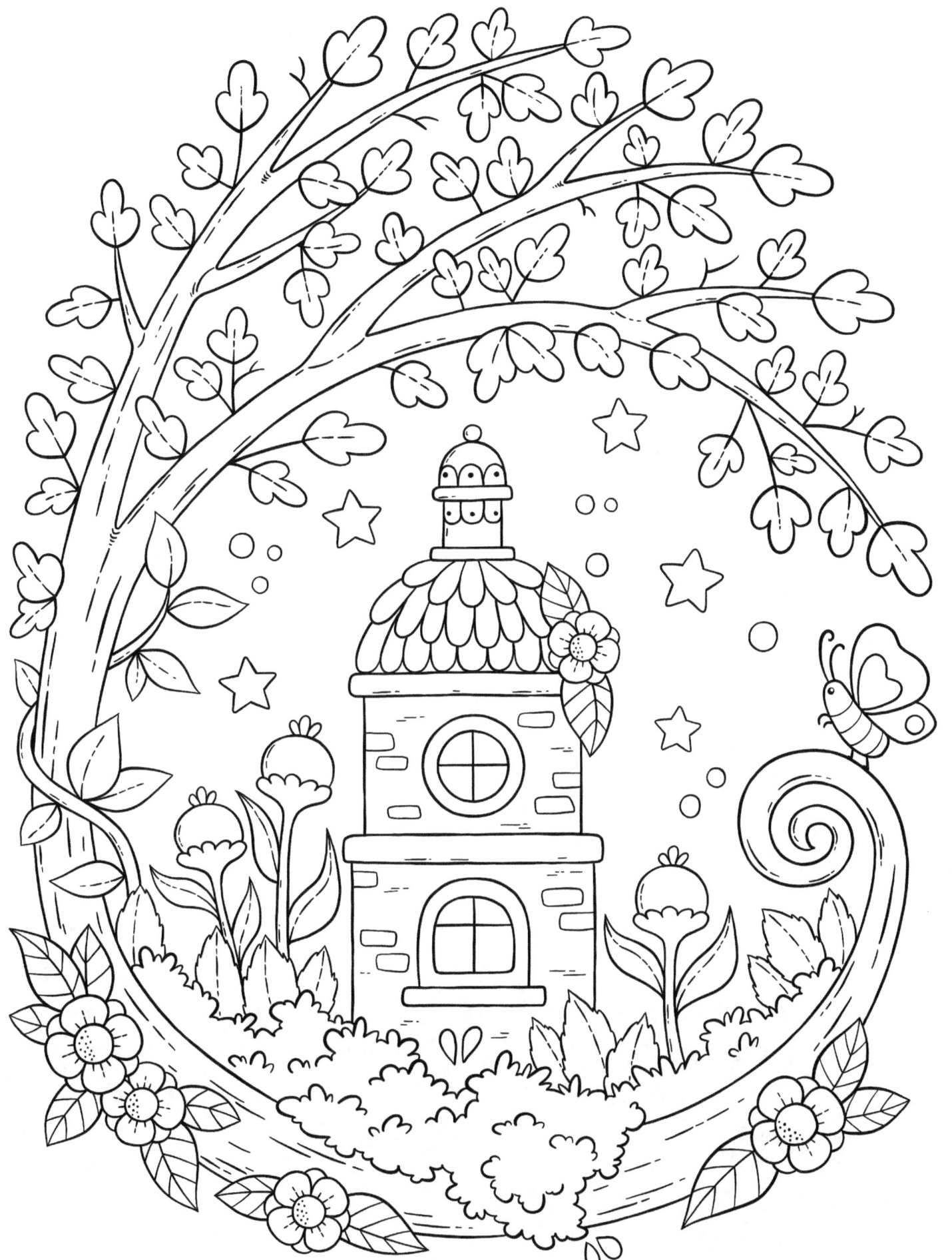

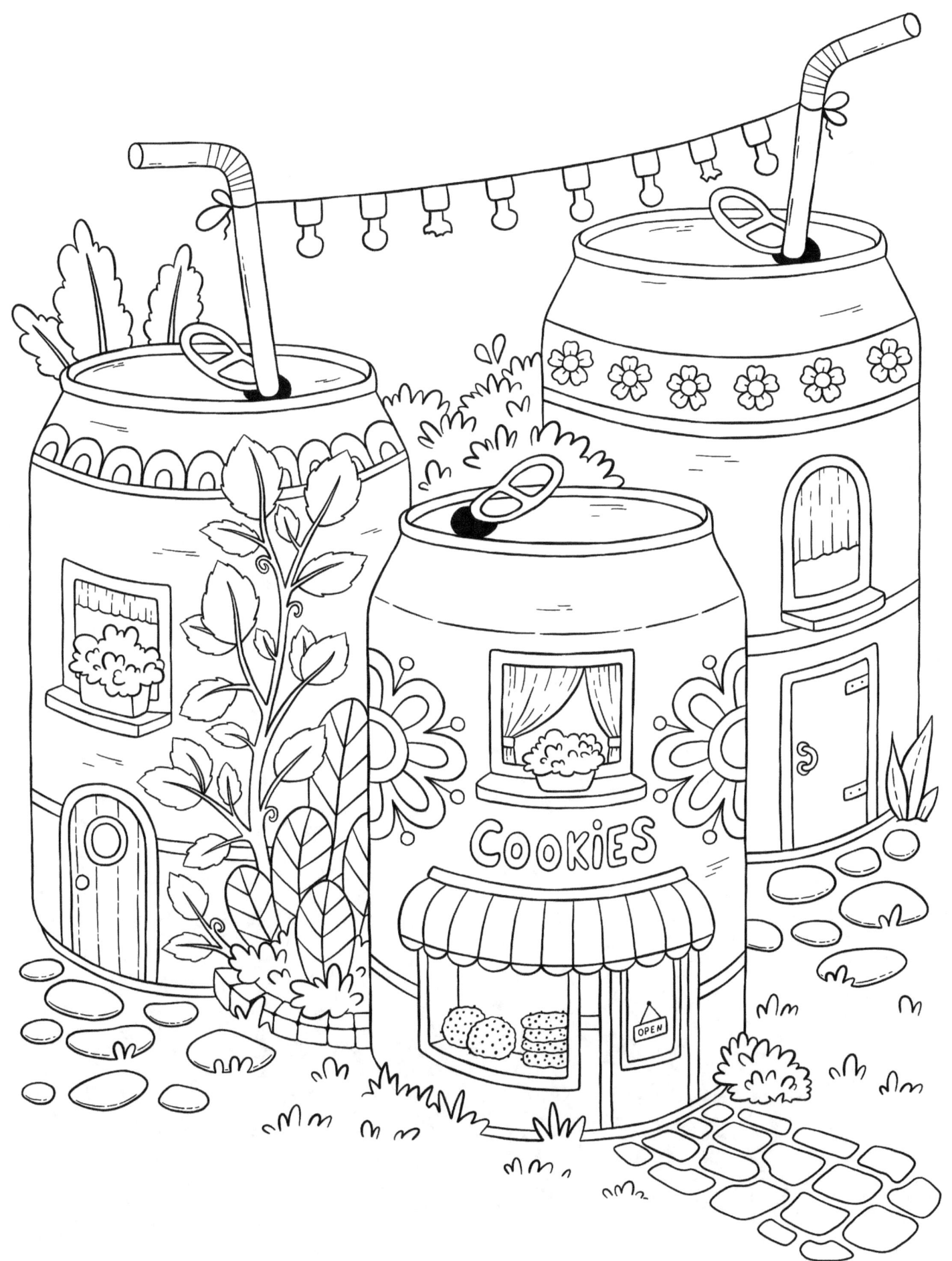

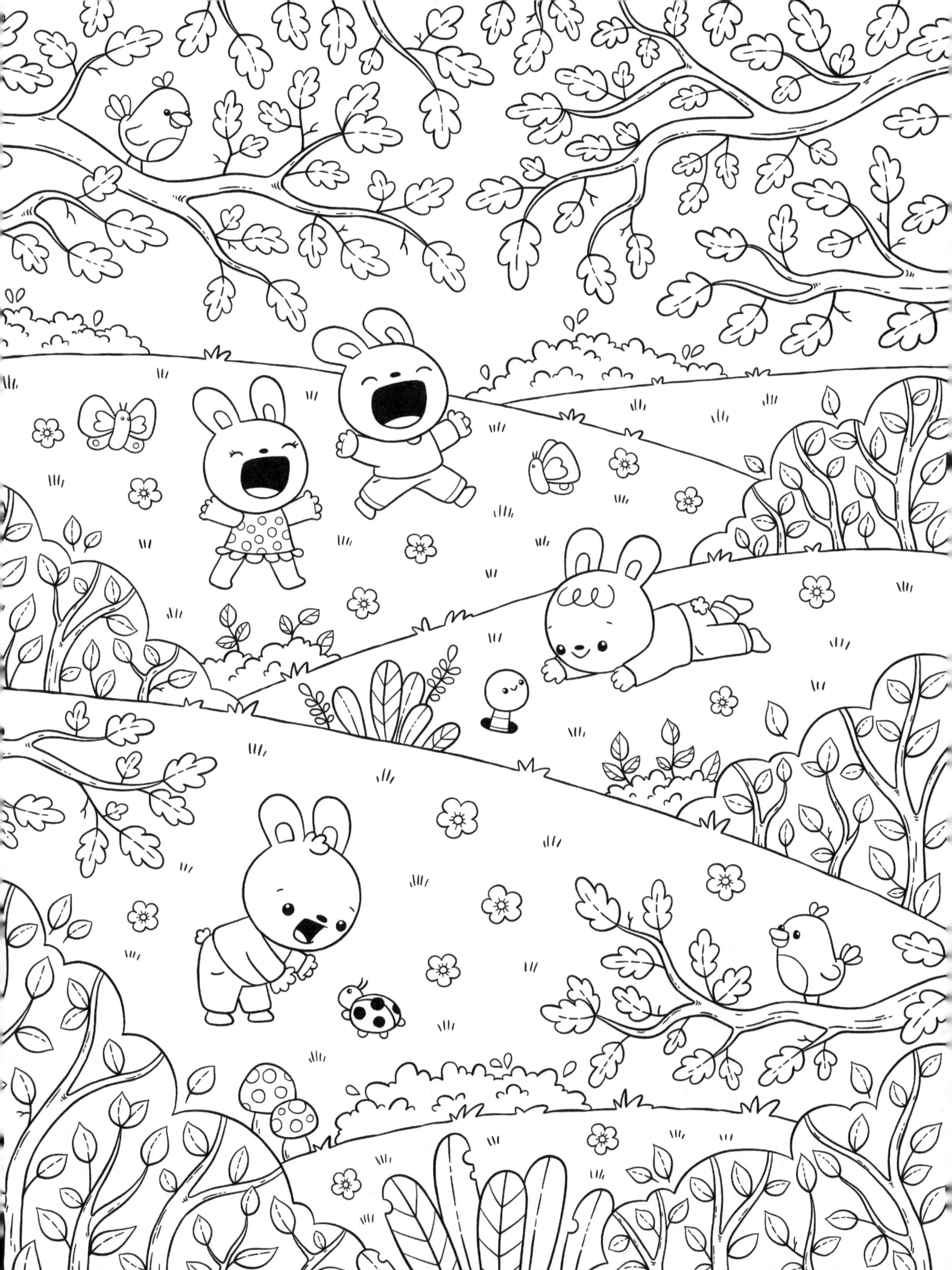

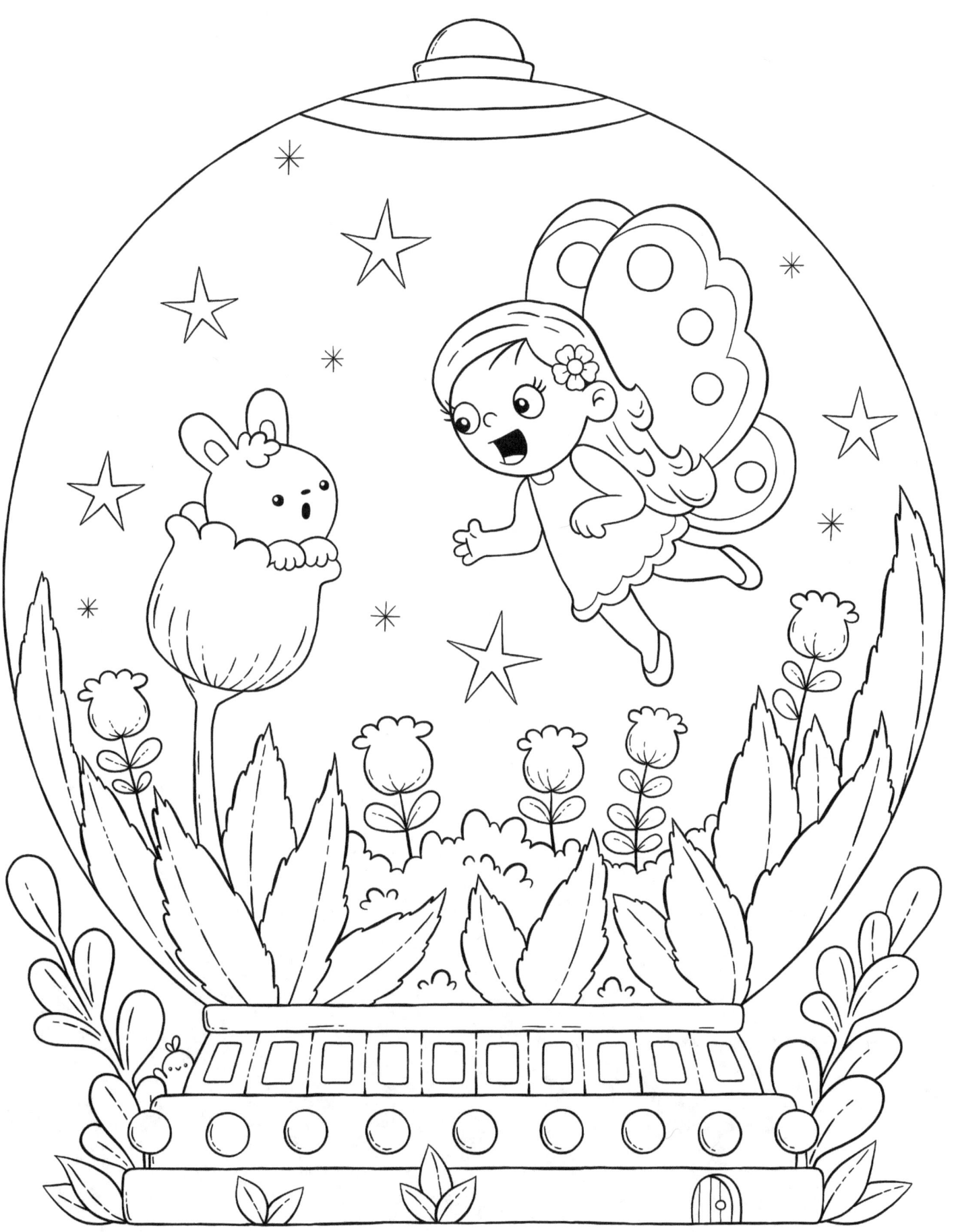

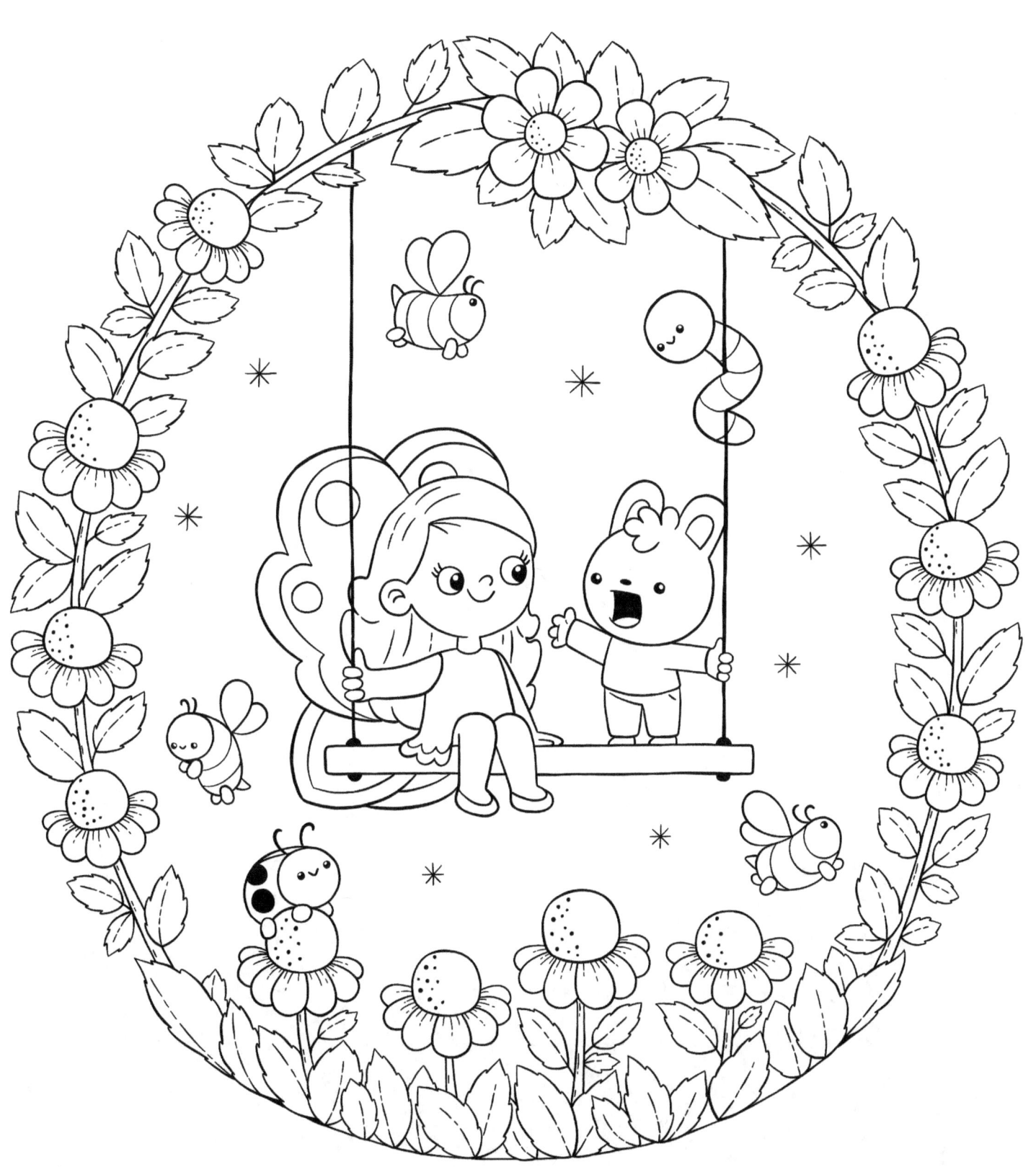

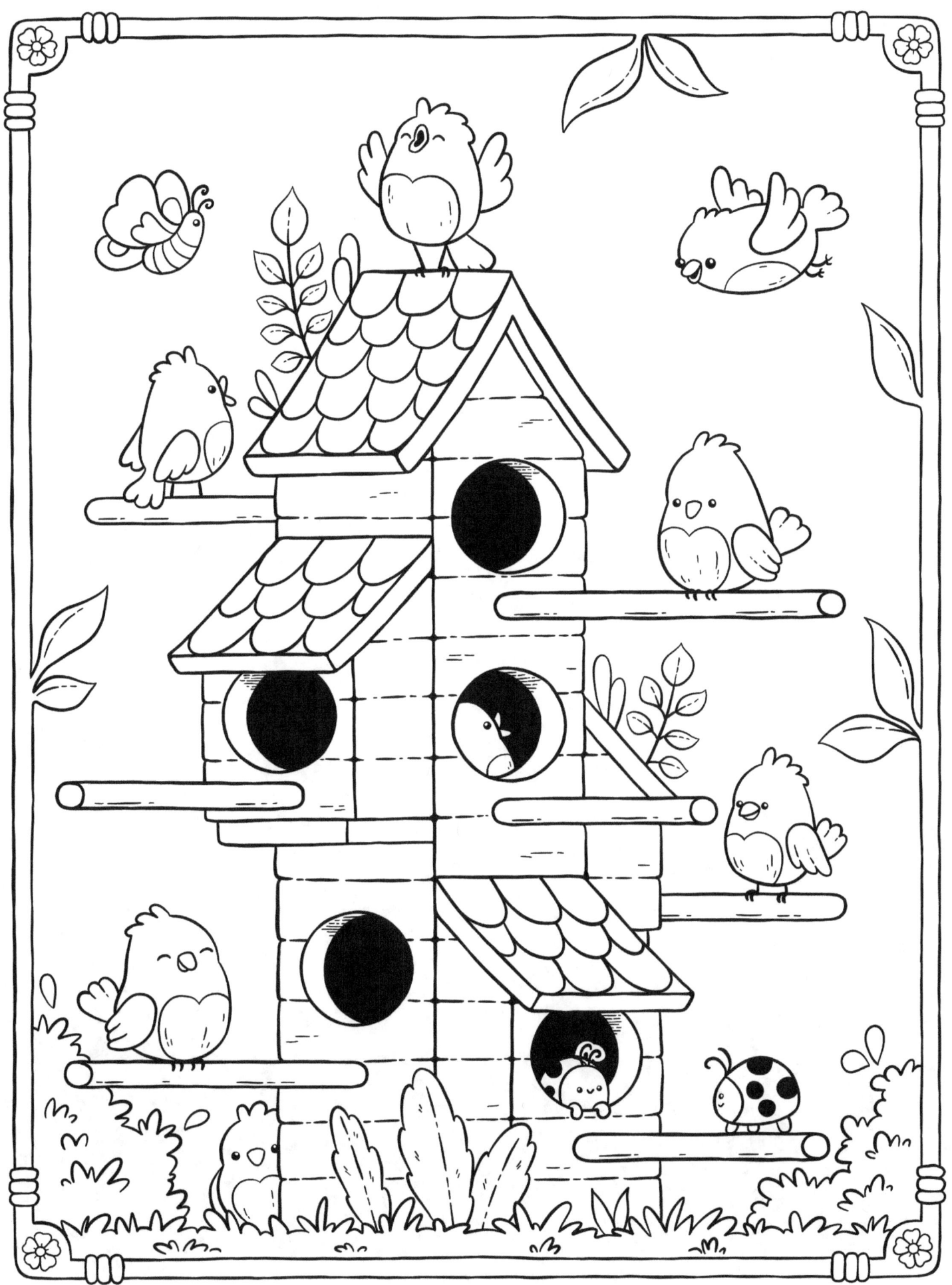

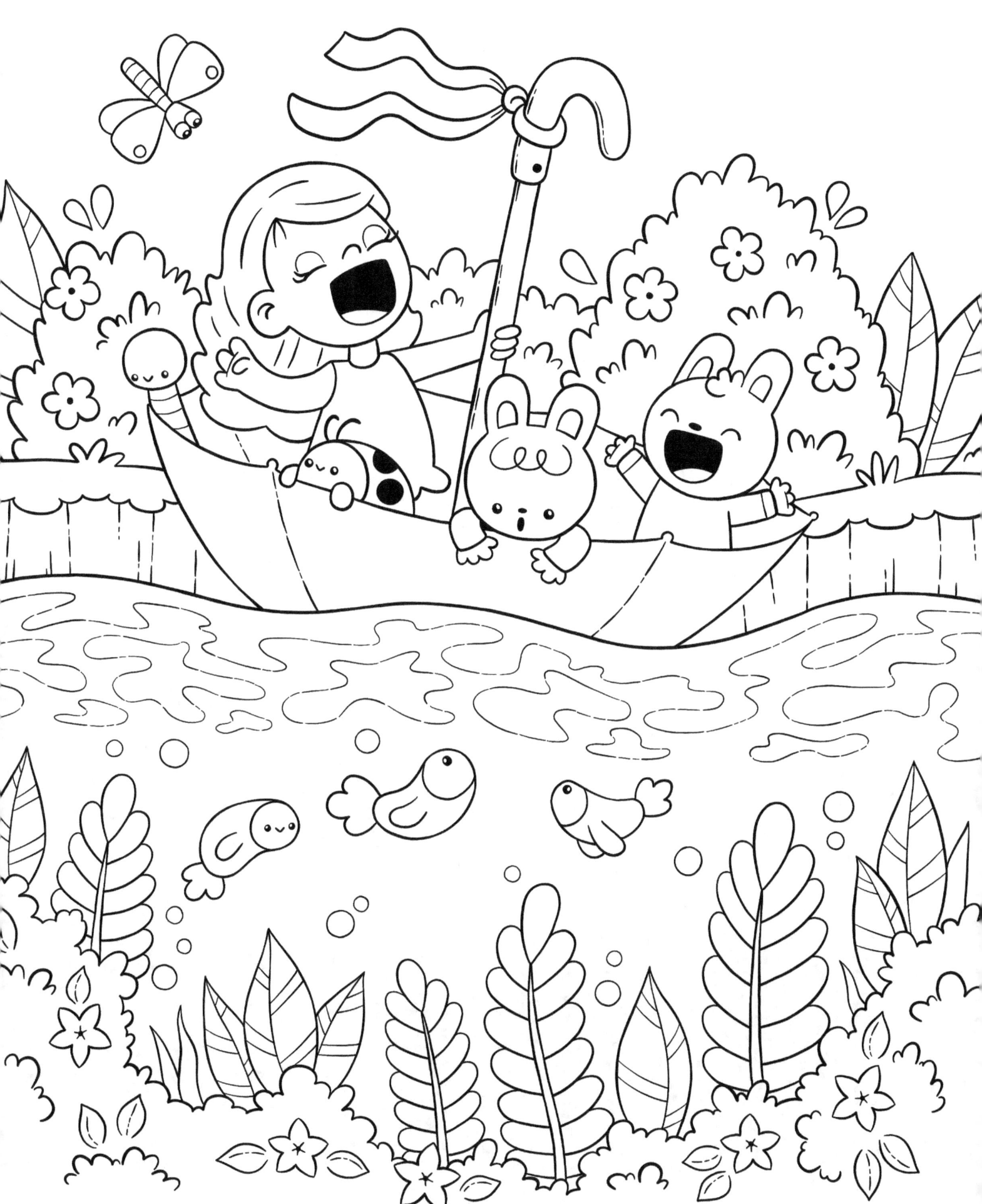

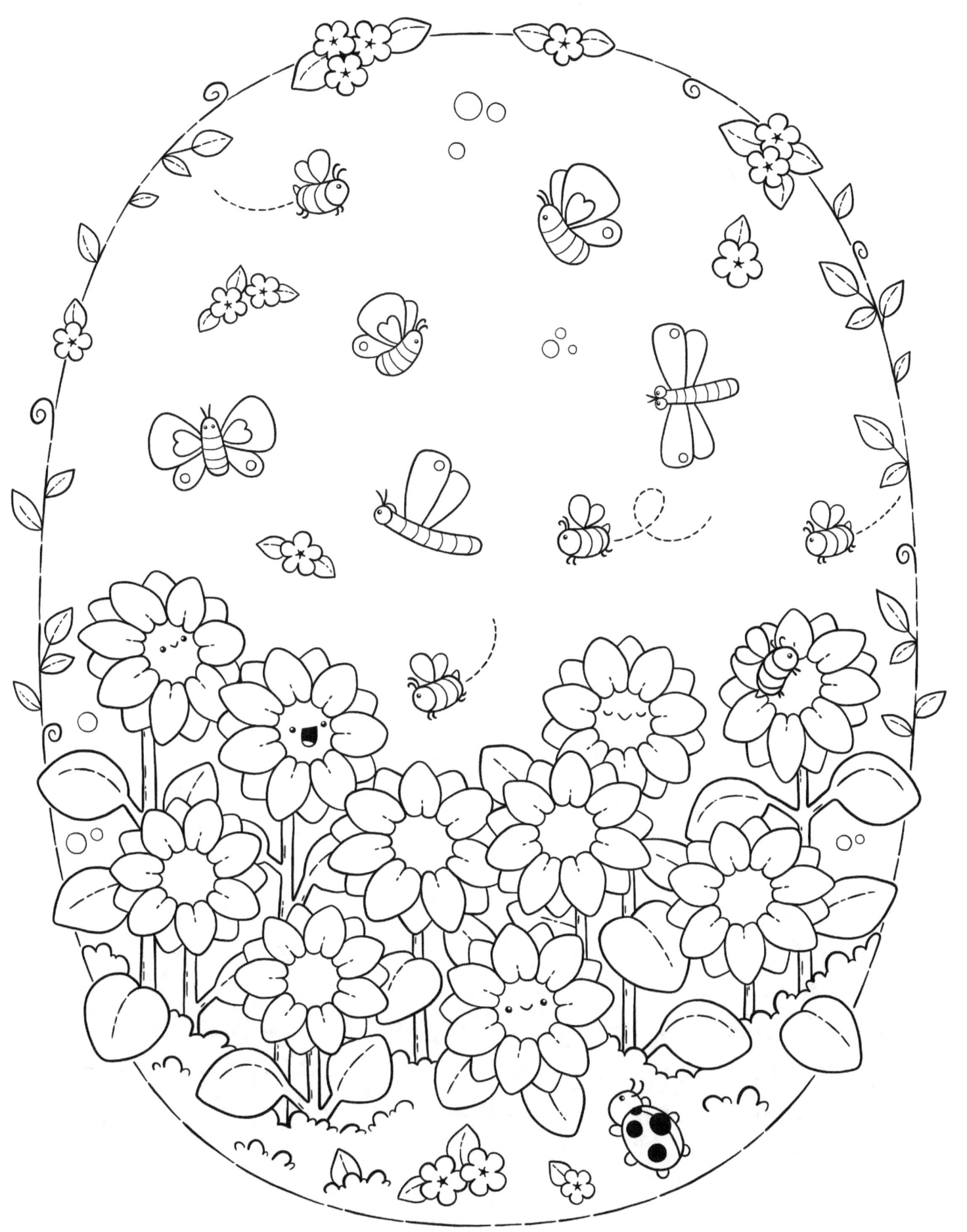

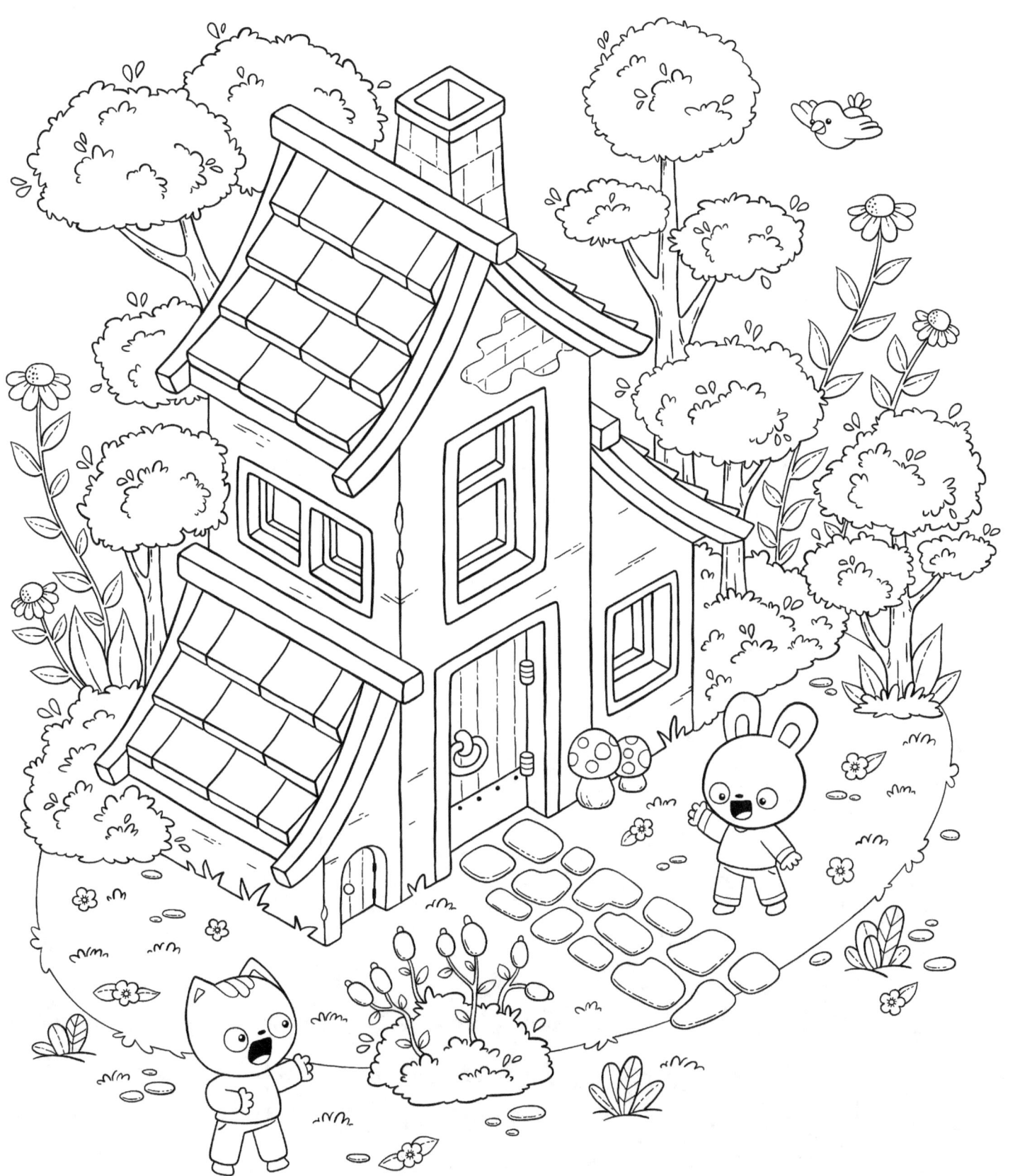

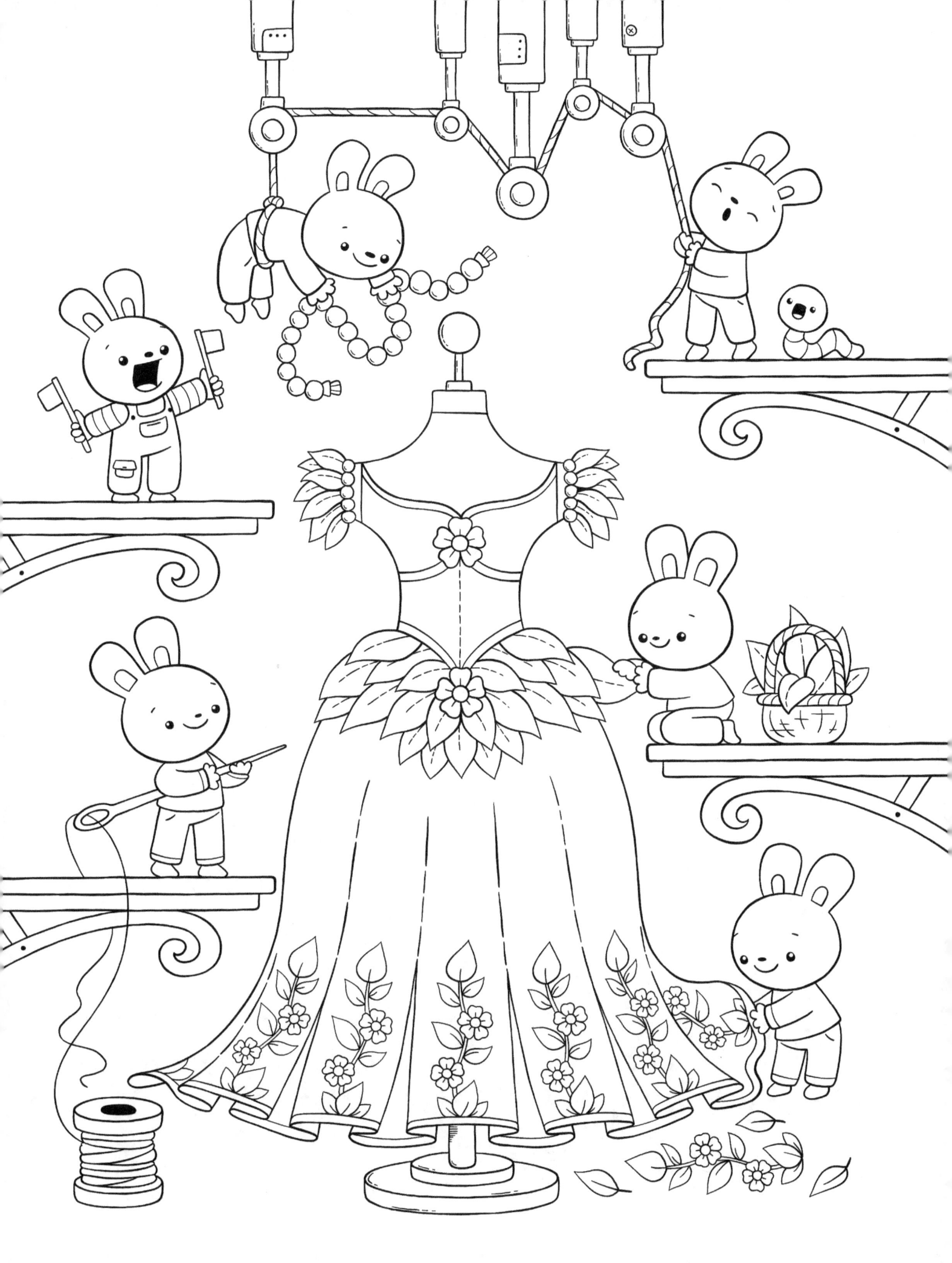

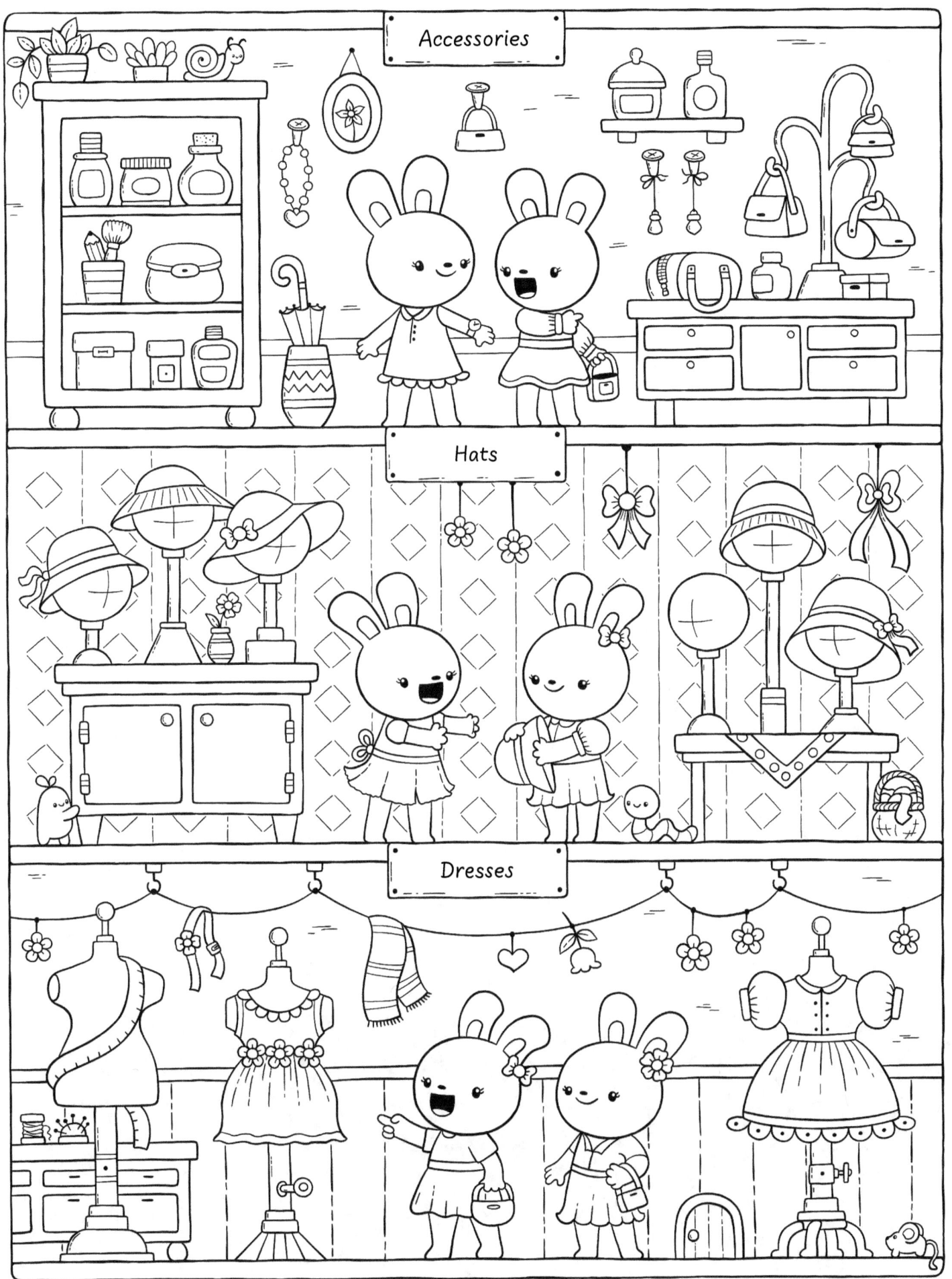

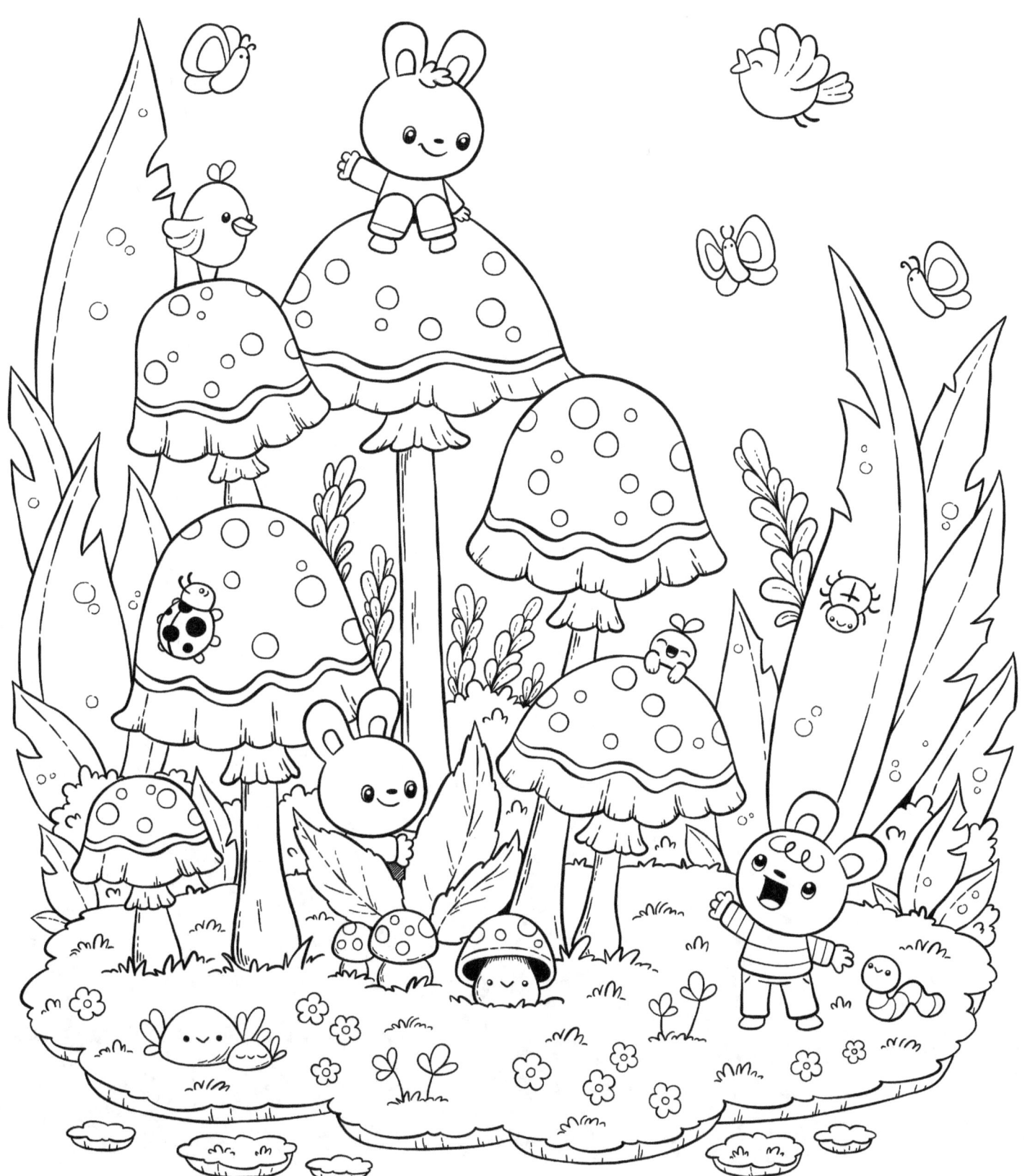

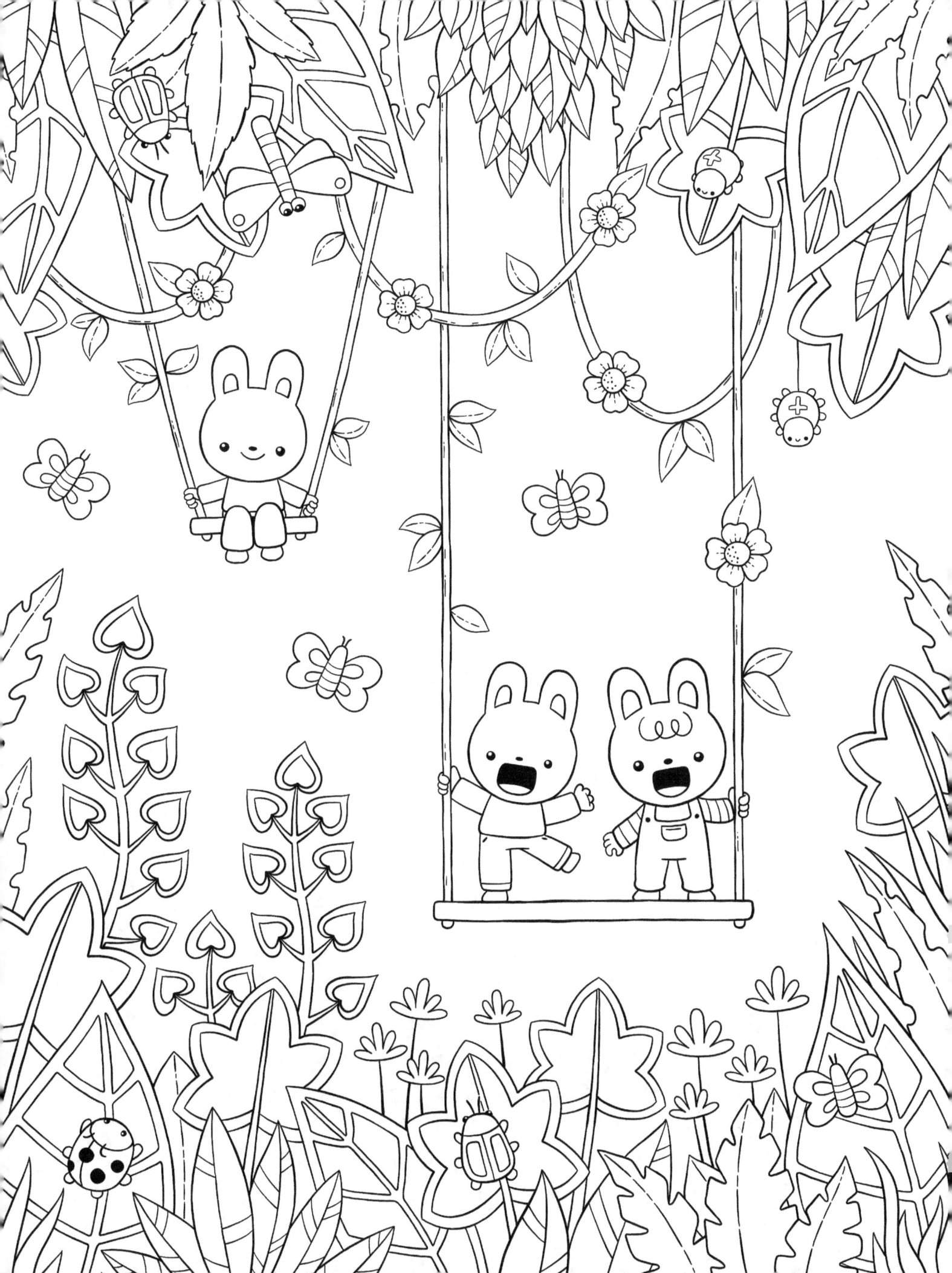

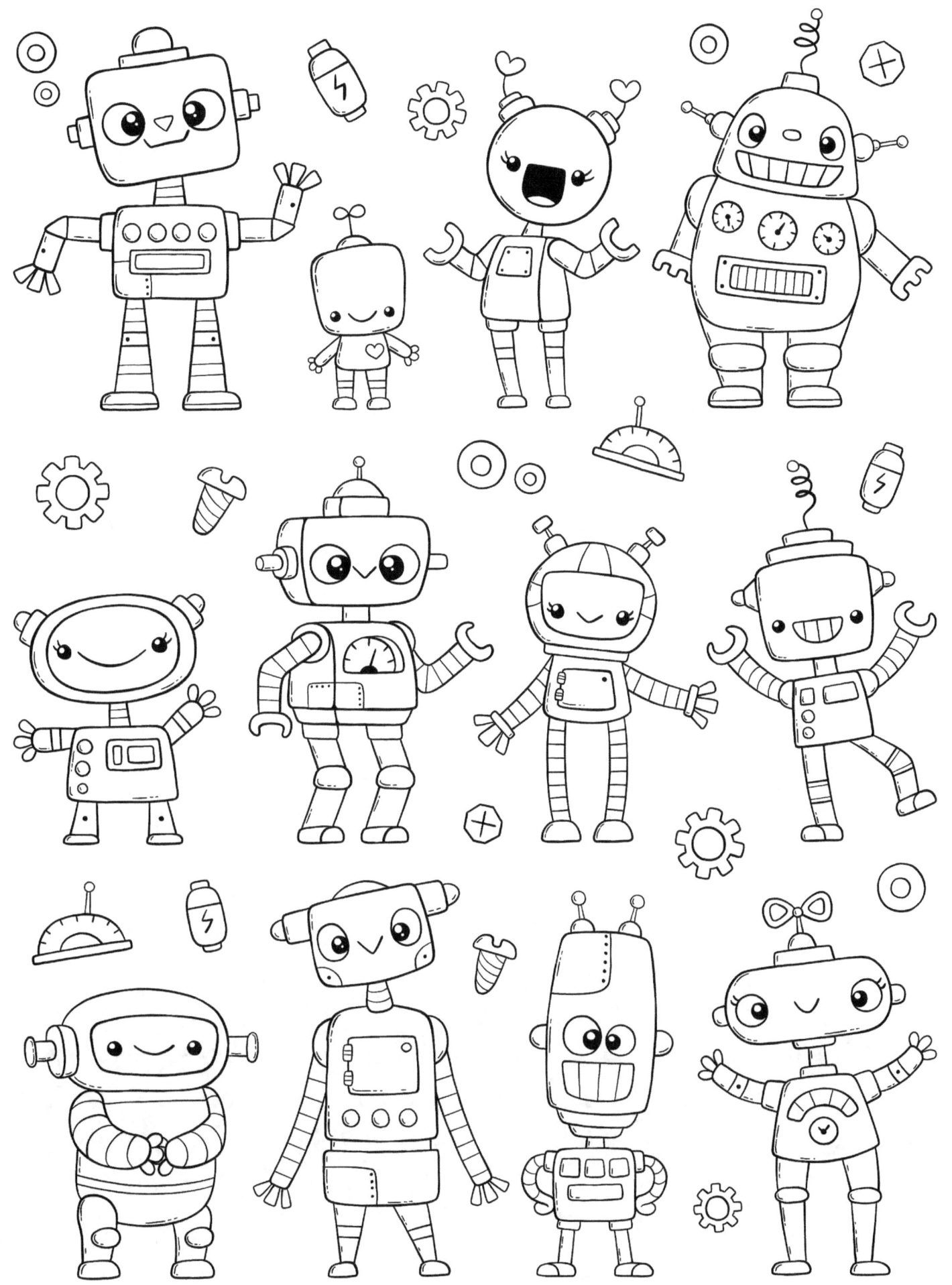

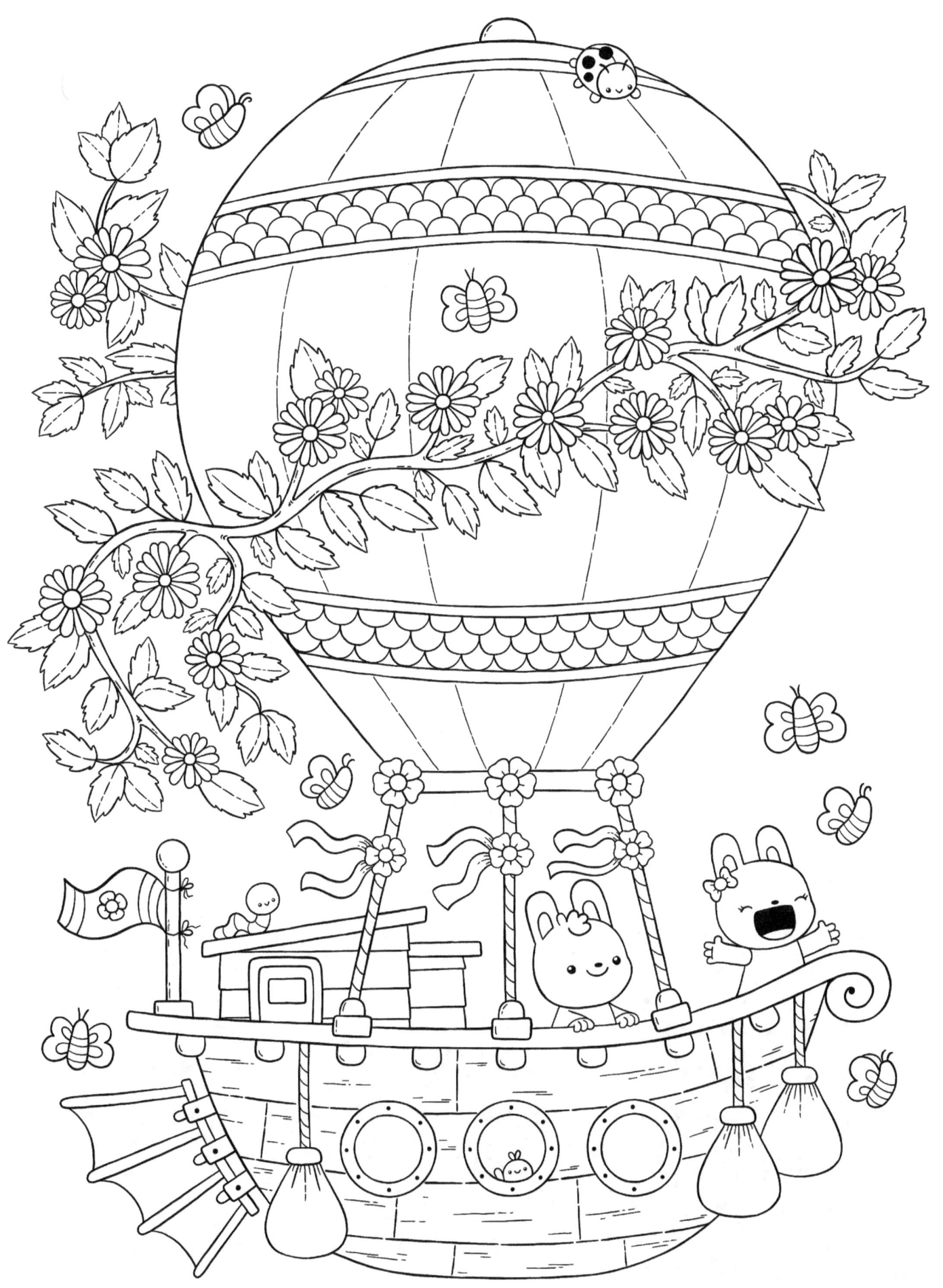

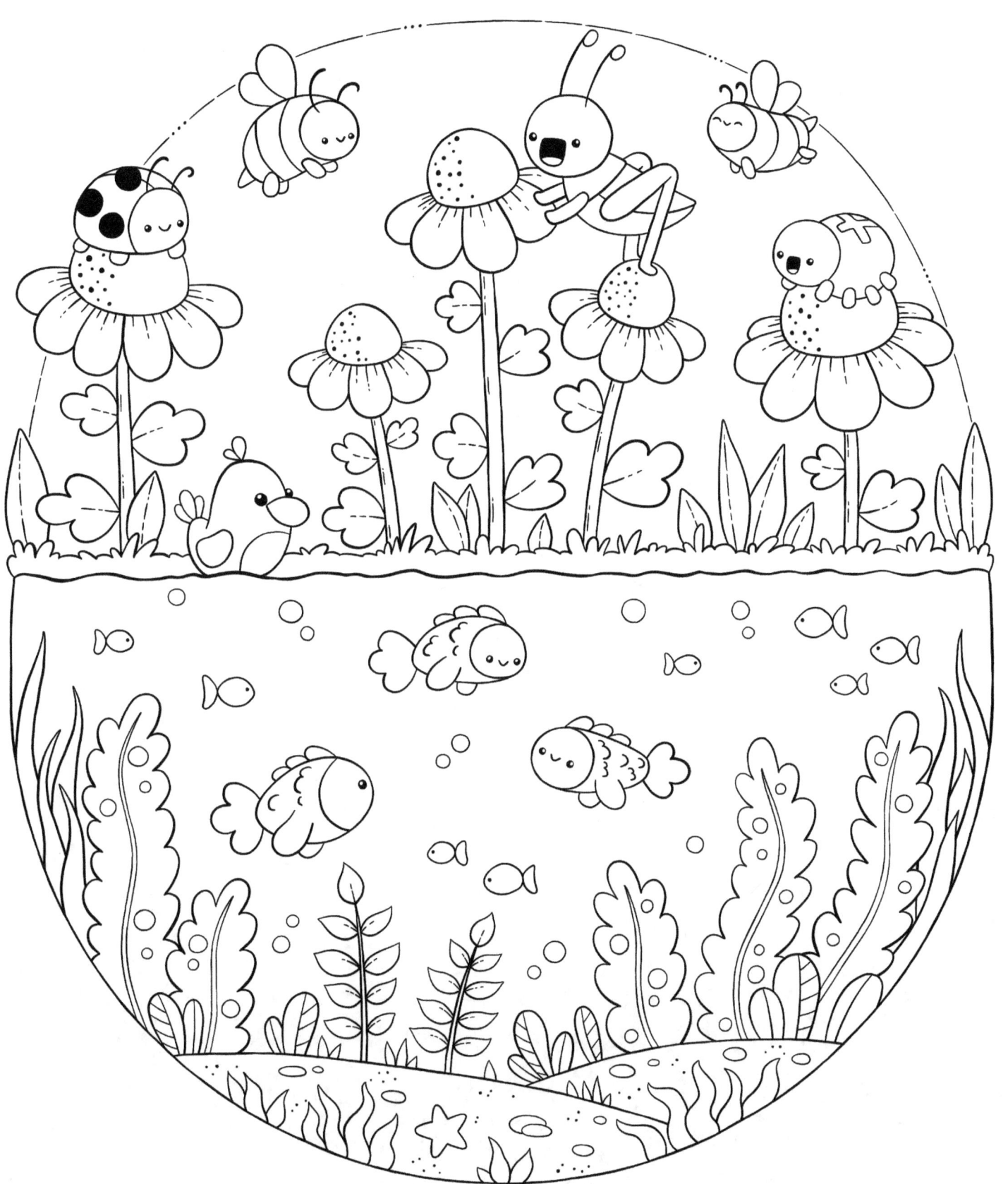

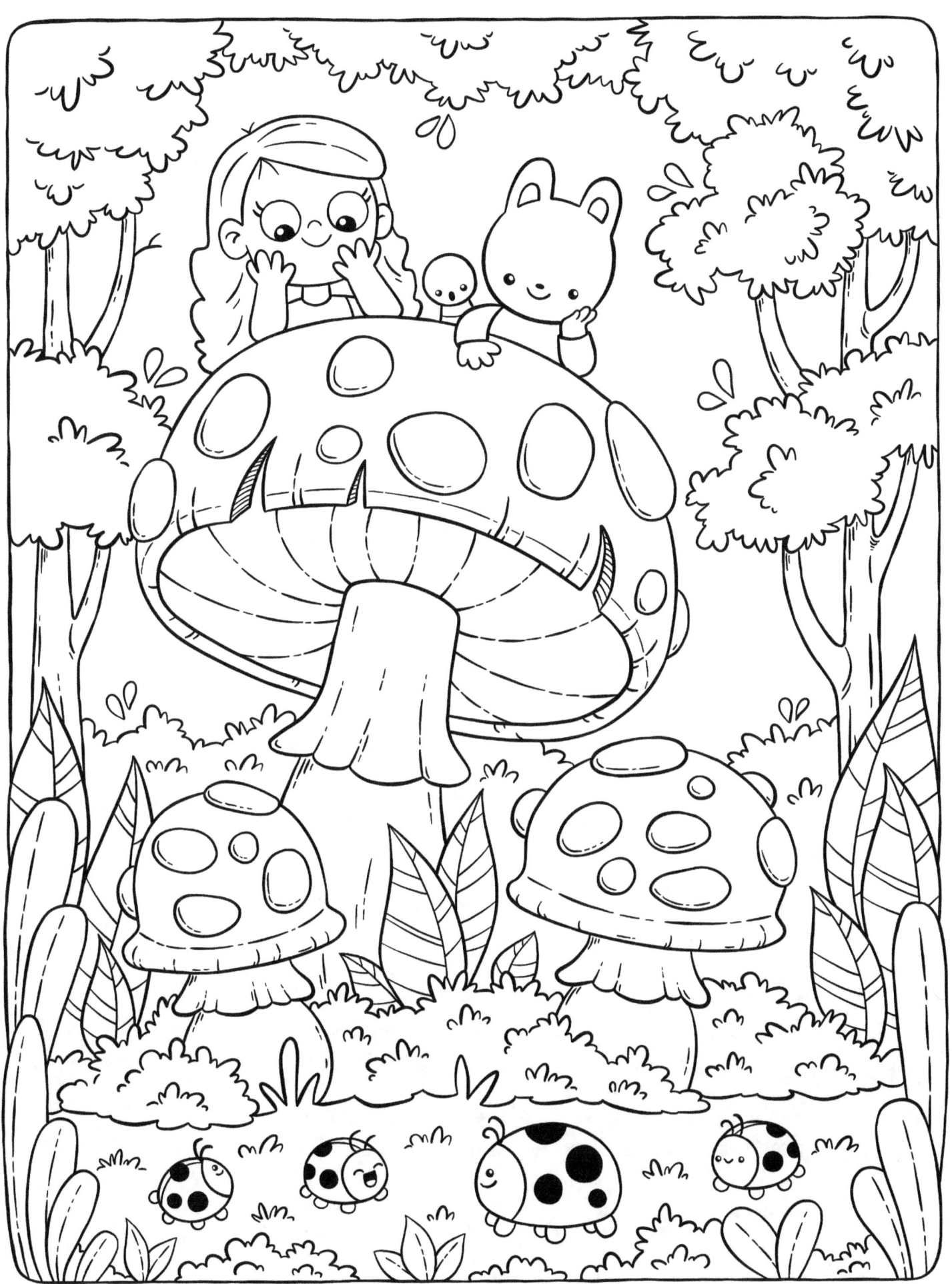

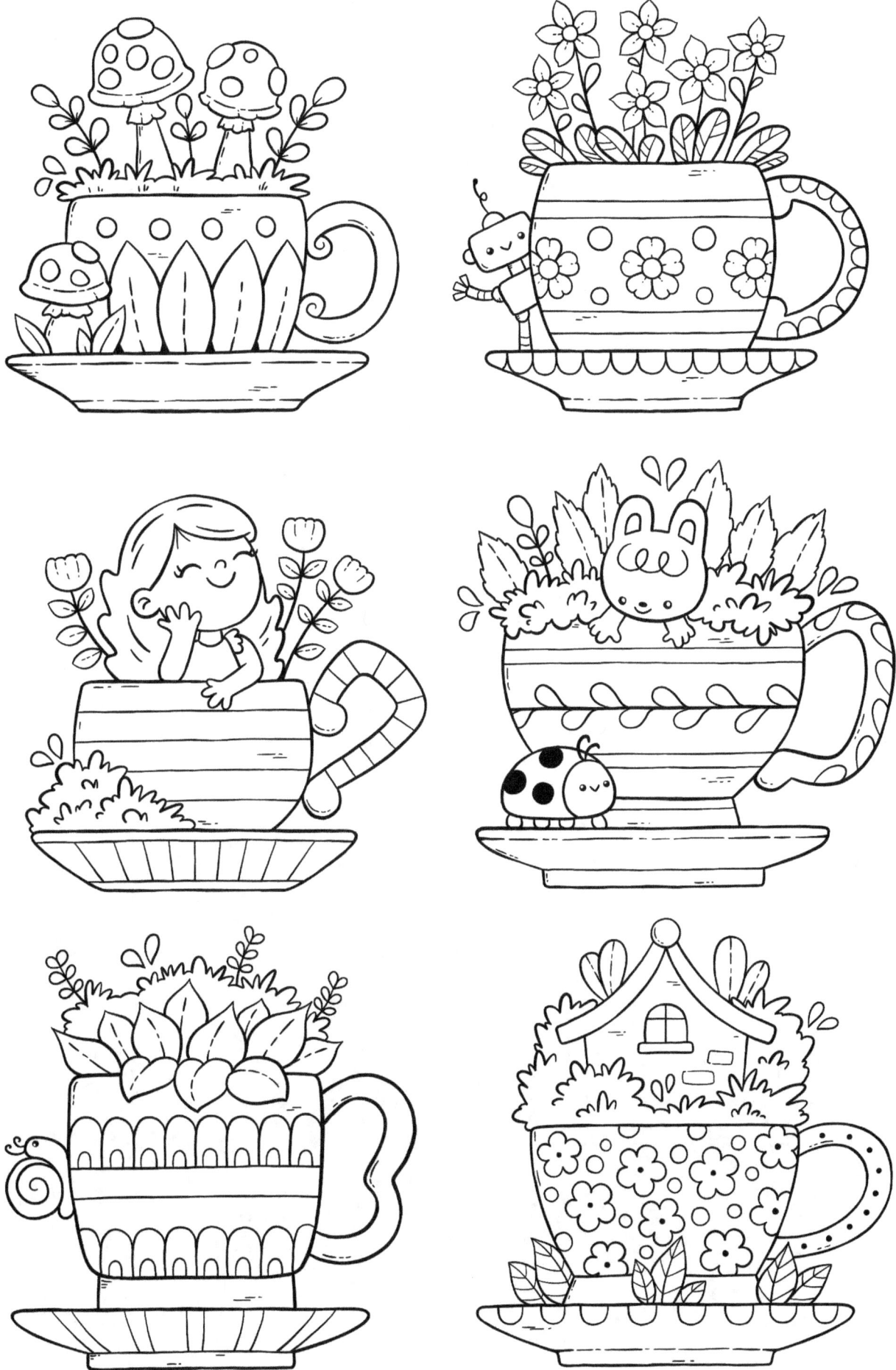

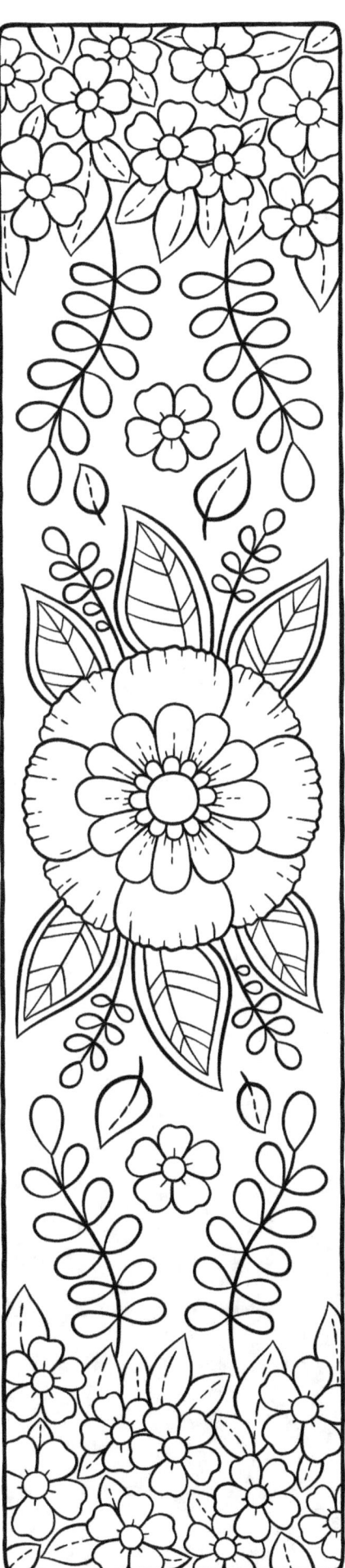

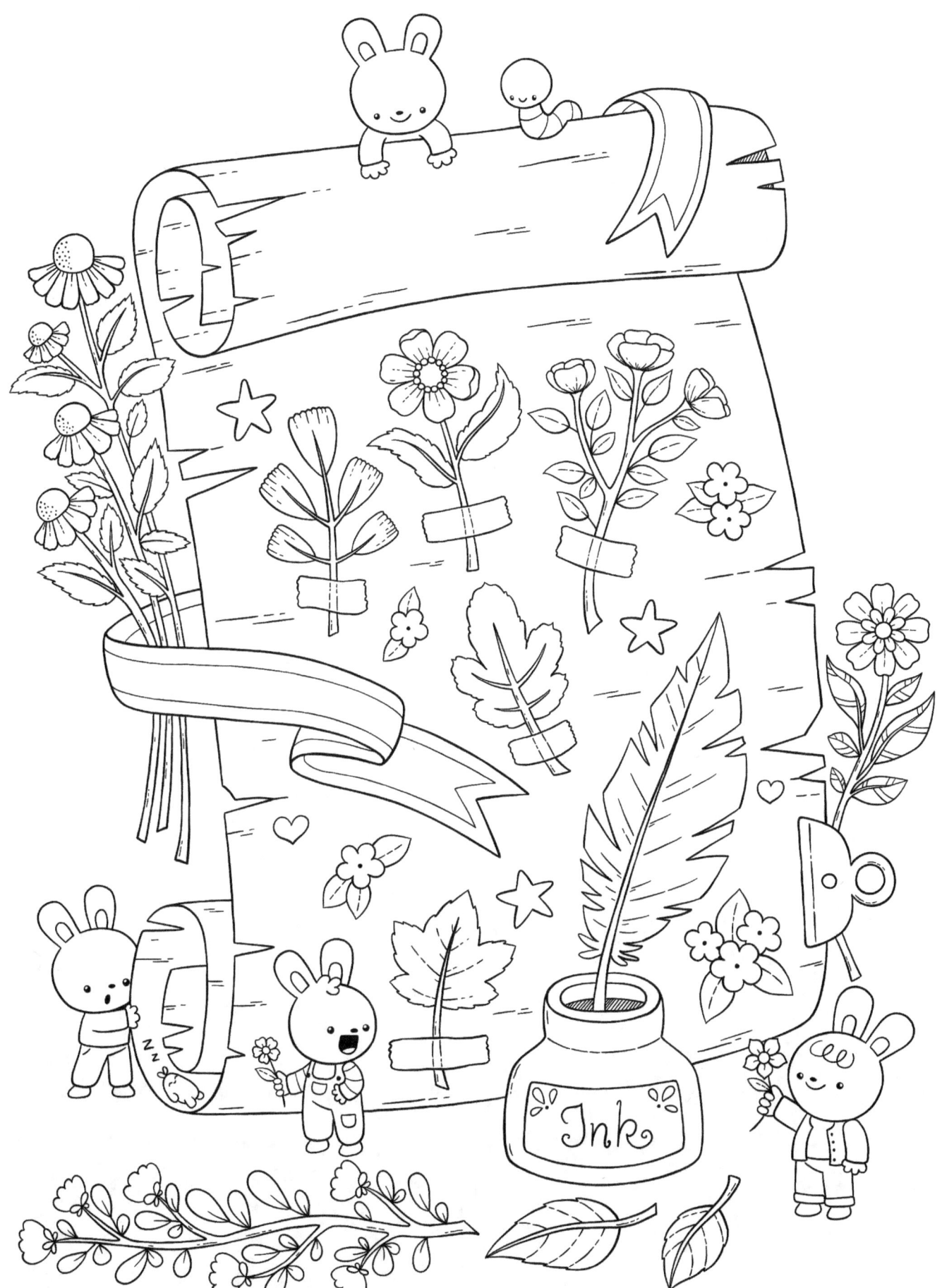

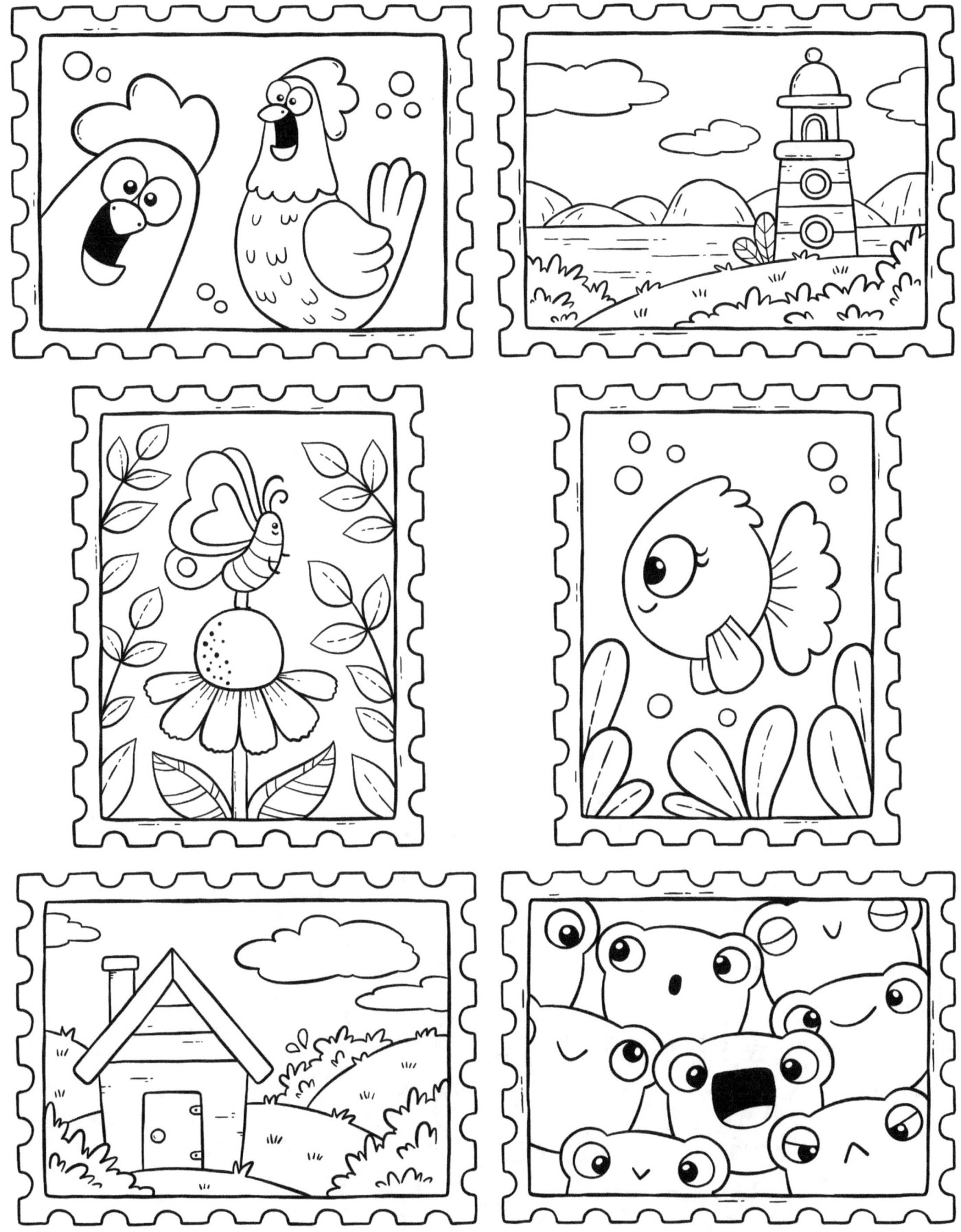

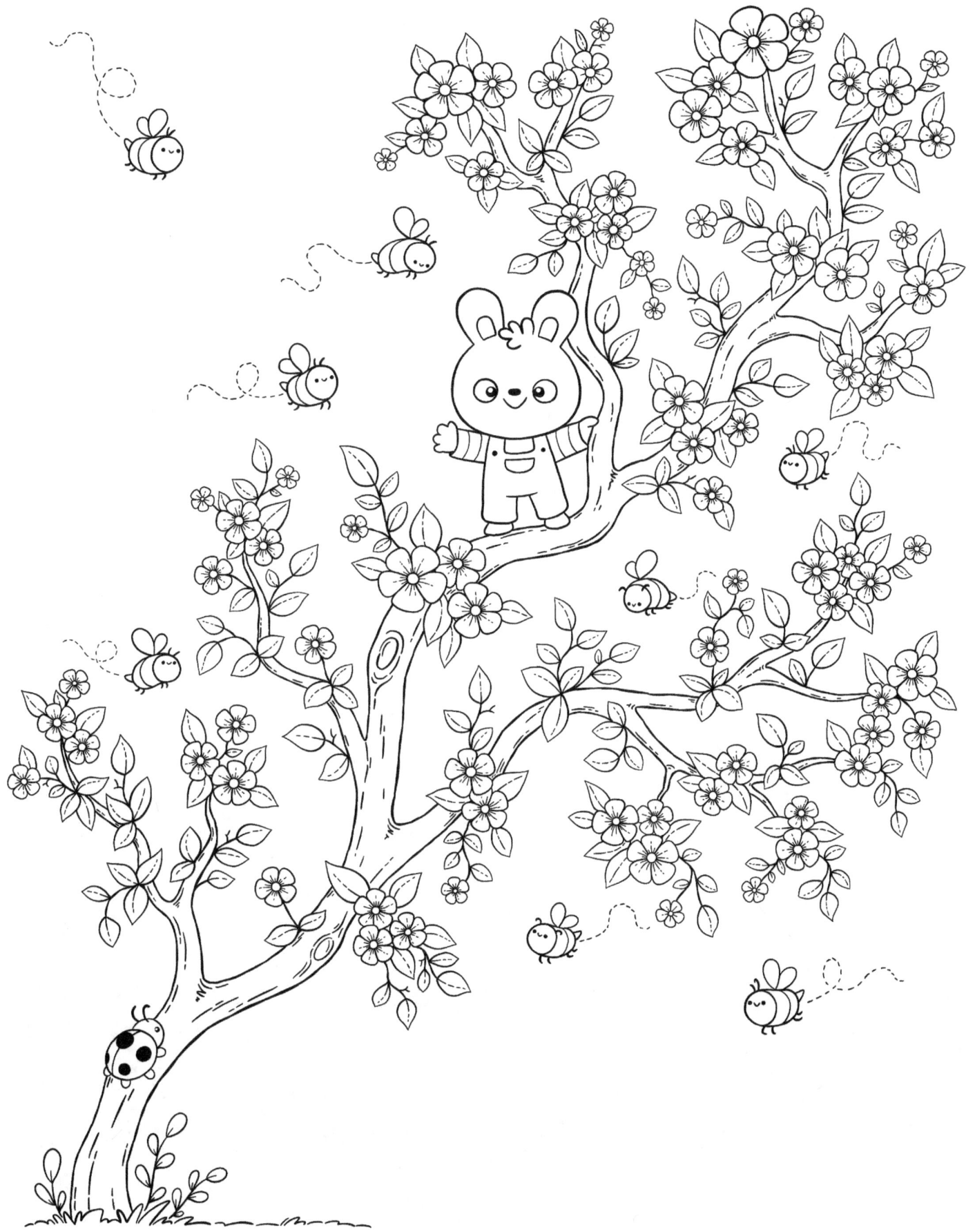

 # Color Test Page

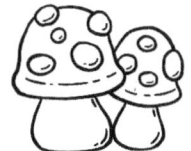 # Color Test Page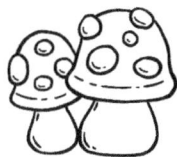

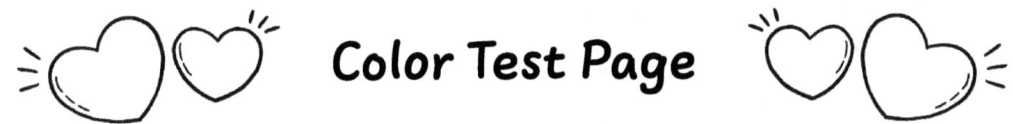
Color Test Page

Color Test Page

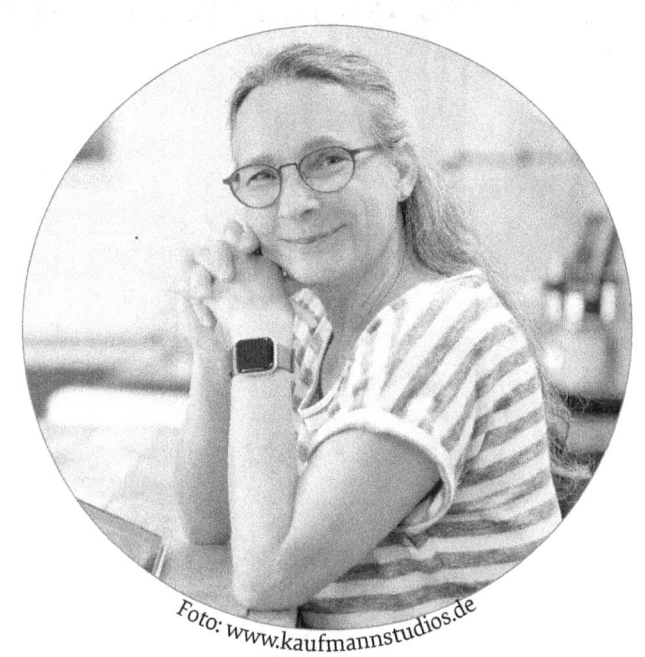

Foto: www.kaufmannstudios.de

We have now reached the end of the book. I hope you enjoyed the pictures and had a lot of fun coloring them. Pleas have a look at my other coloring books. You can find information about them on the following pages, on my website, on Amazon or on social media.

www.gabiwolf.de
hello@gabiwolf.de

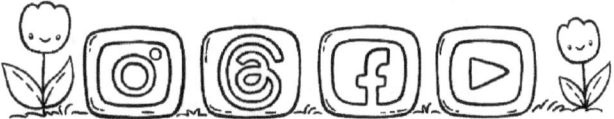

@gabisgrafiken

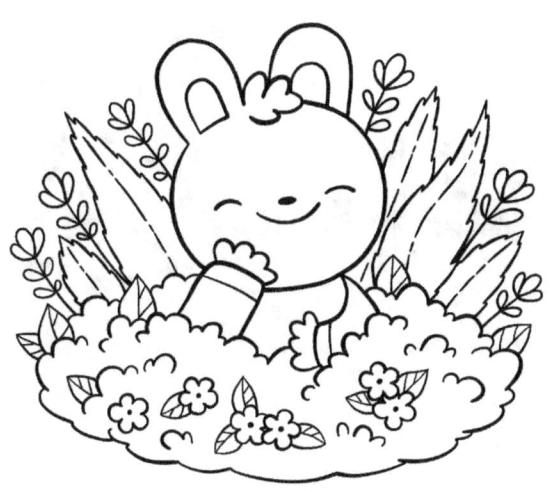

More Coloring Books from Gabi Wolf

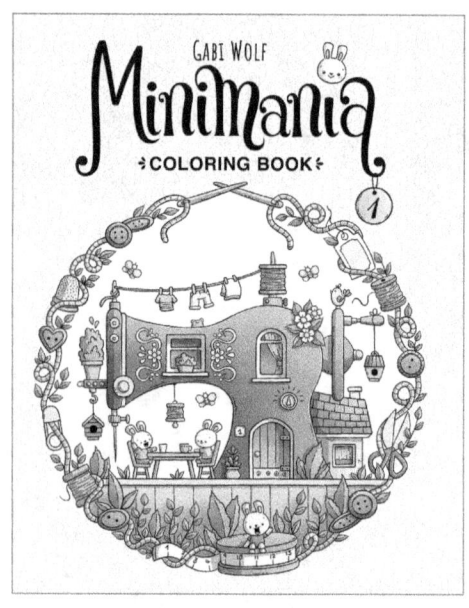
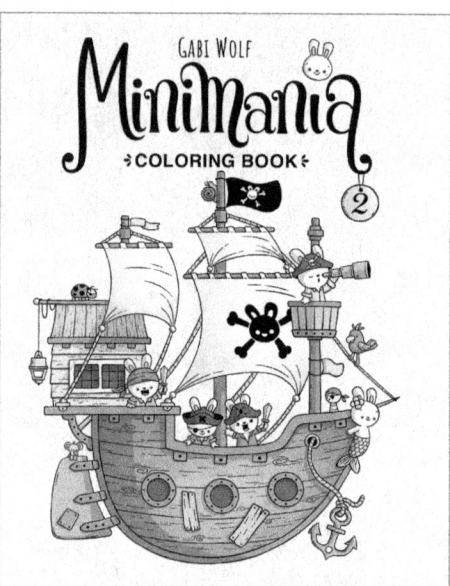
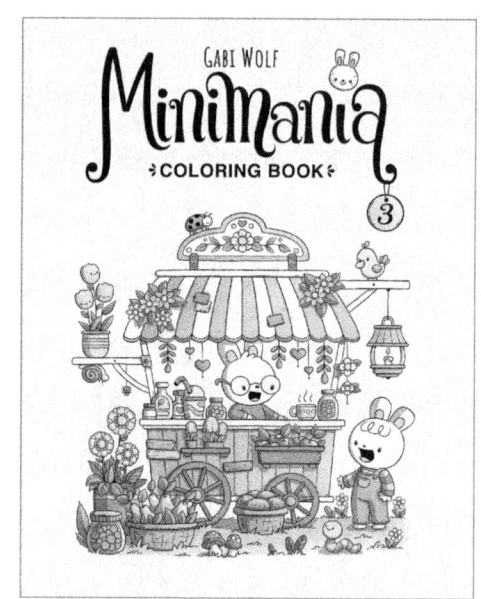
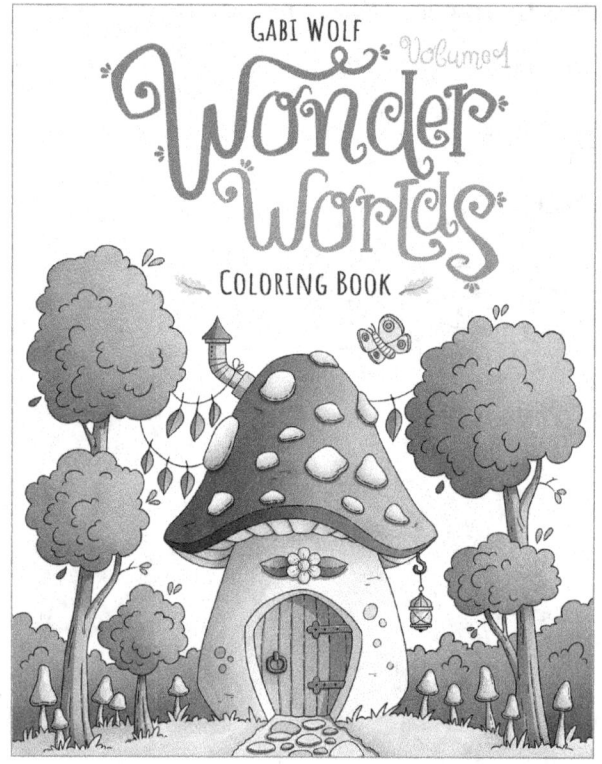
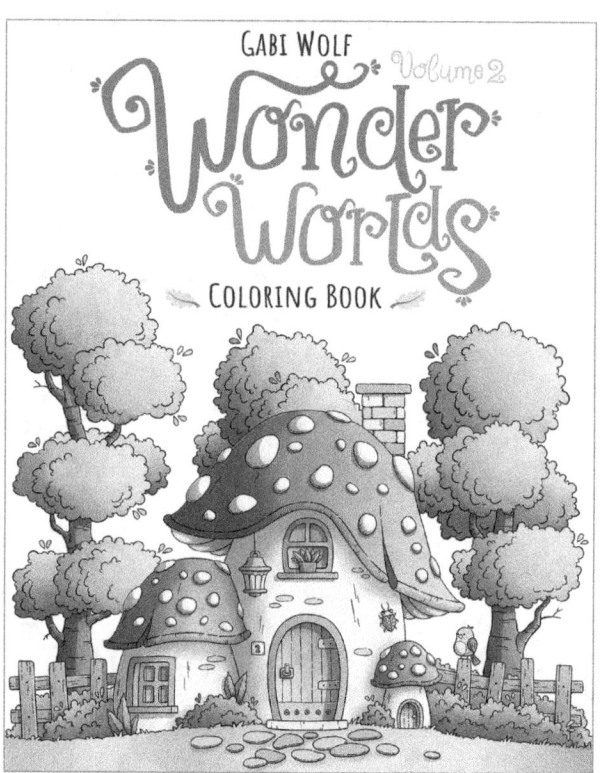

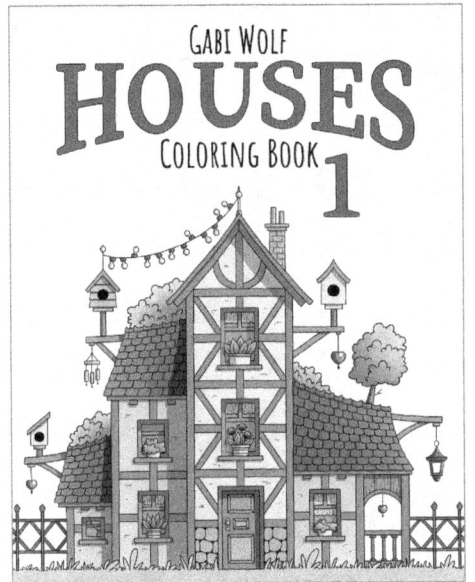
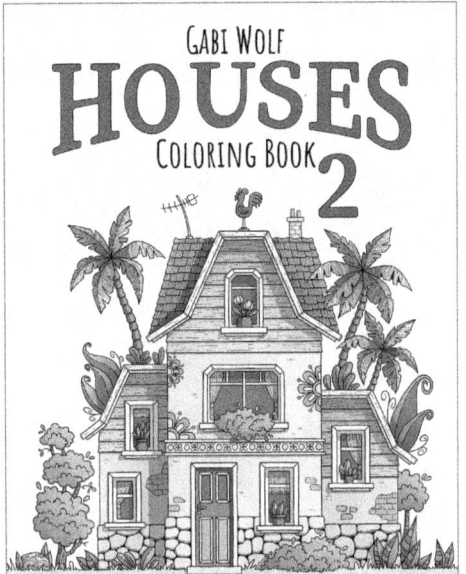
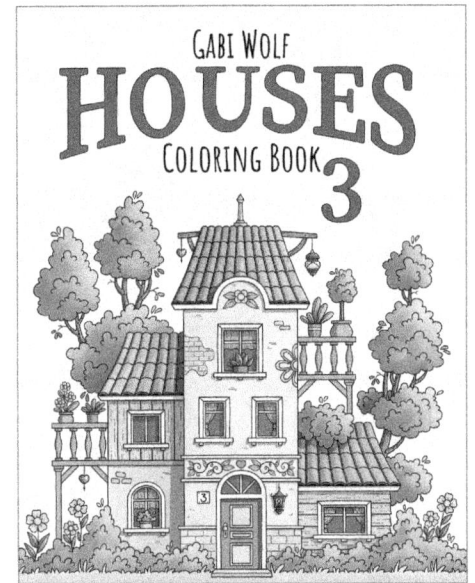
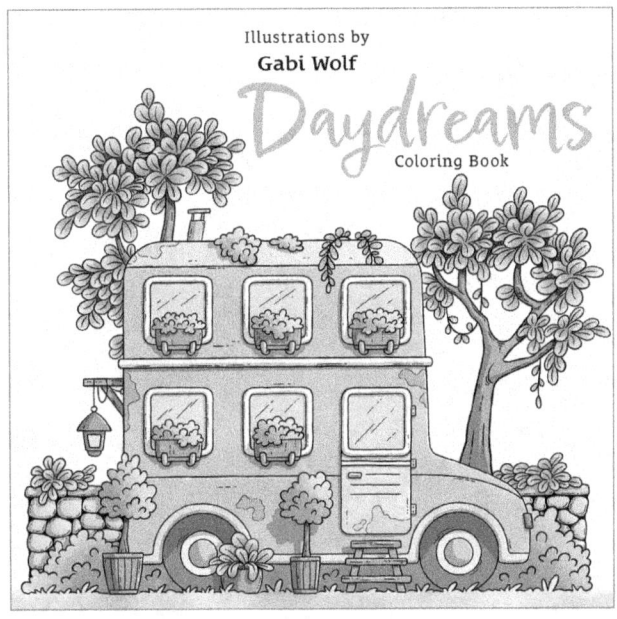
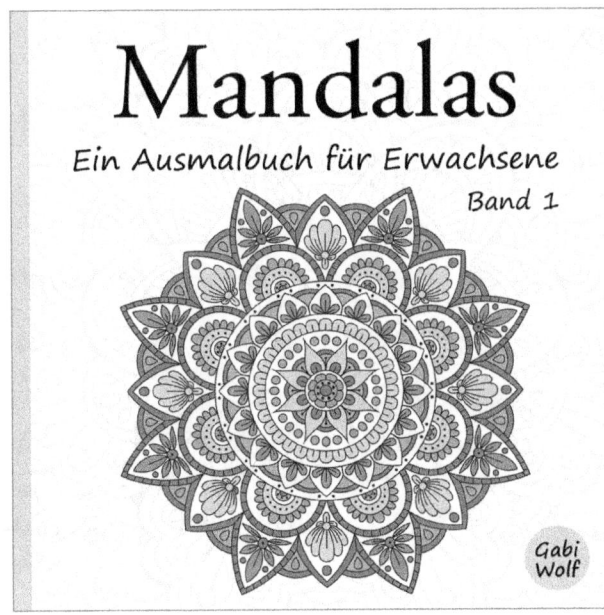
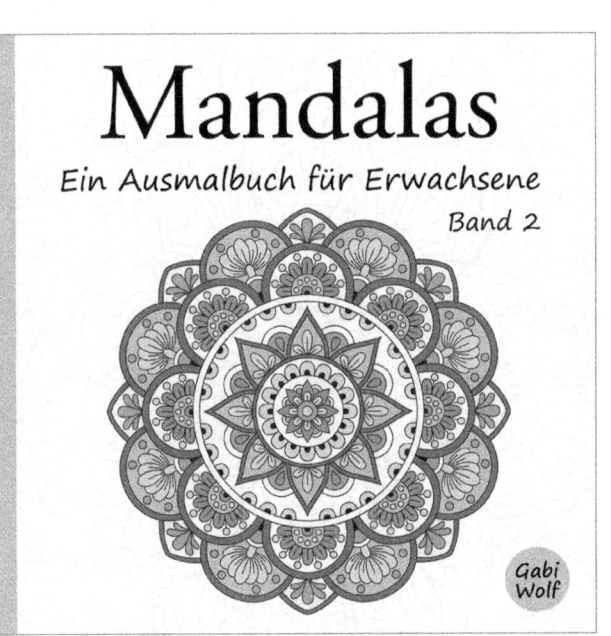

Copyright © 2024 Gabi Wolf, Berlin
Cover & Illustrationen: Gabi Wolf
All rights reserved
Theodor-Brugsch-Str. 2, 13125 Berlin
Germany

www.ingramcontent.com/pod-product-compliance
Lightning Source LLC
Chambersburg PA
CBHW062120220526
45471CB00010B/3809